Tattoo Flash Book Two
Artwork by: David Lee Lough

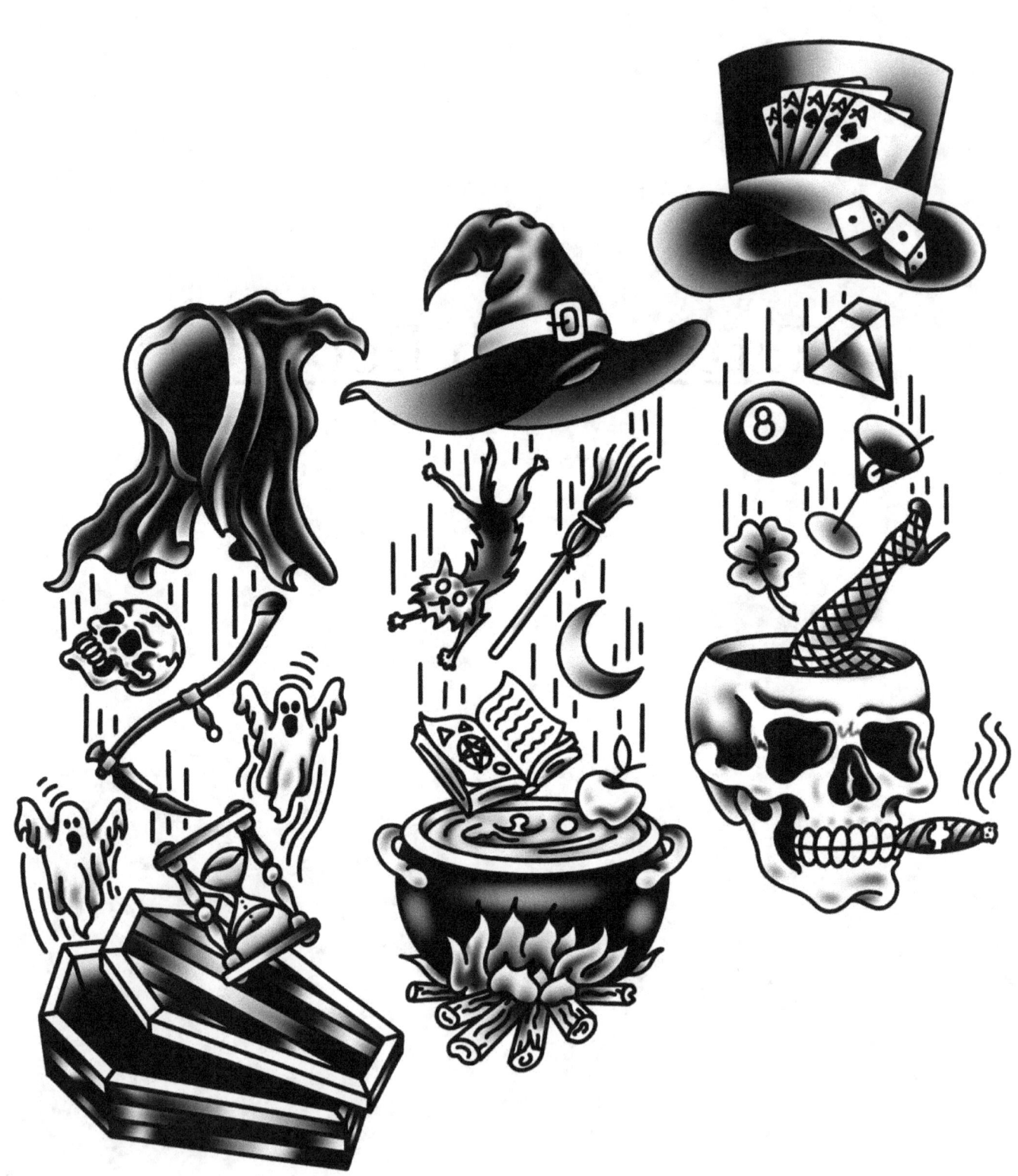

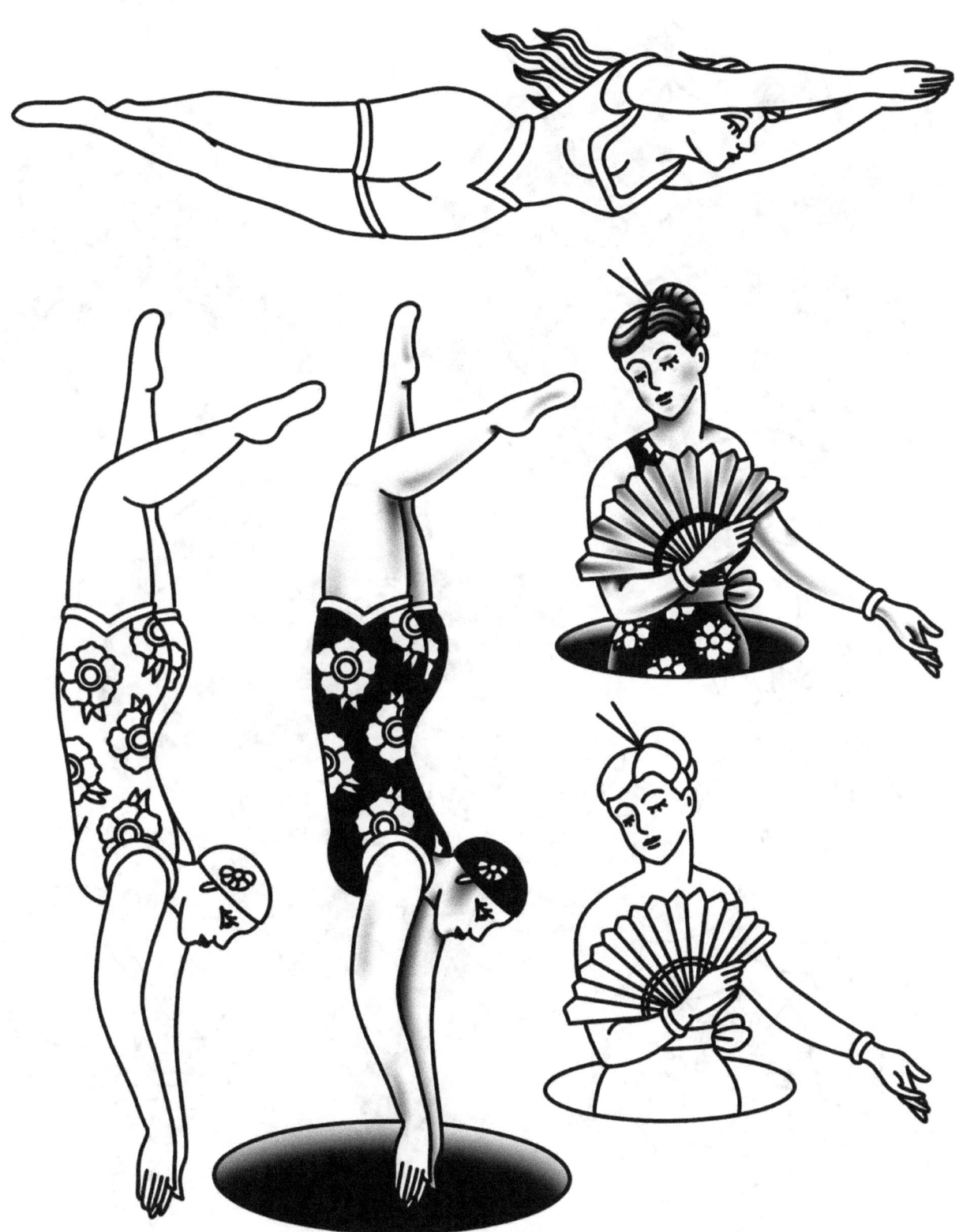

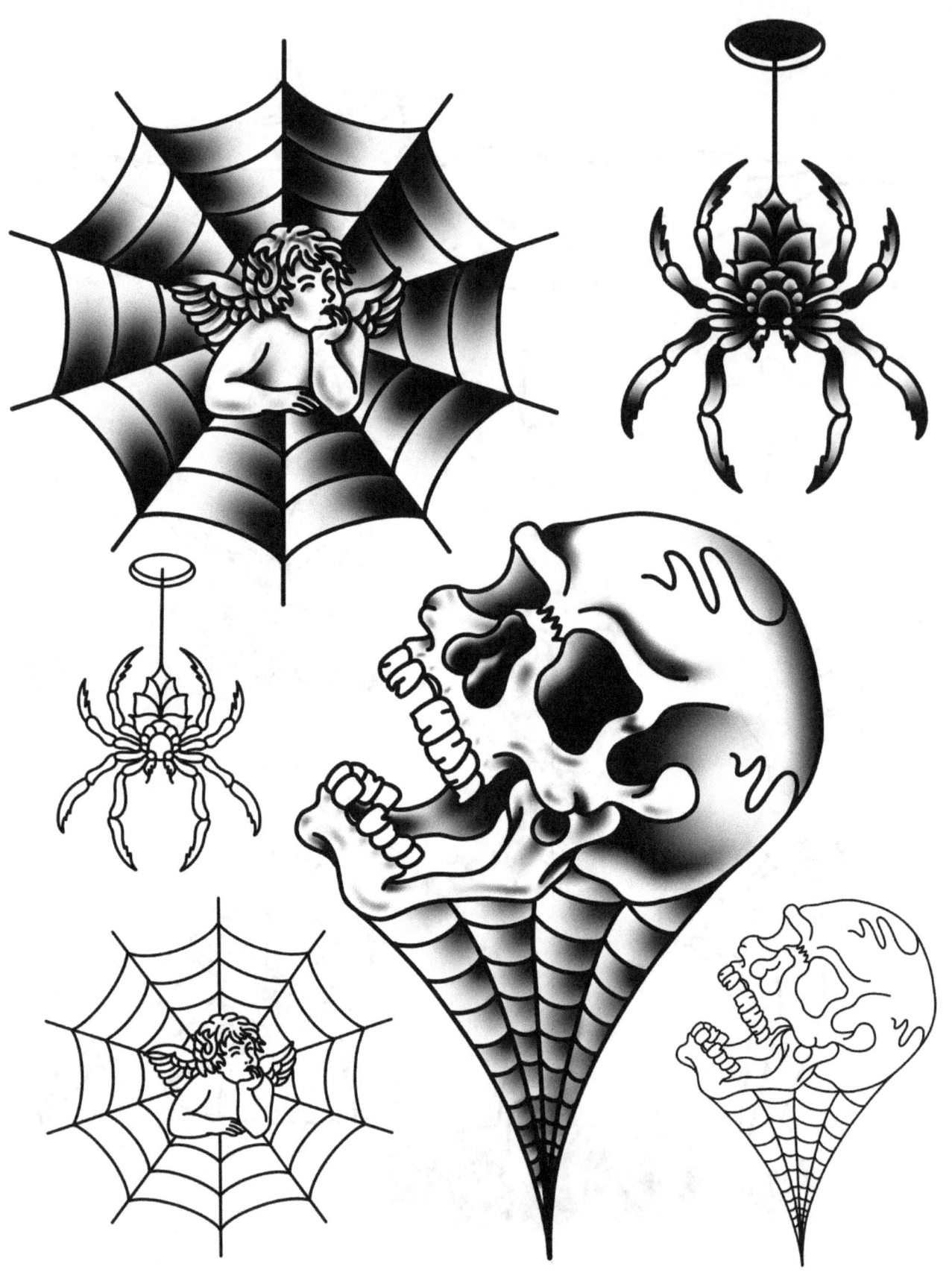

Celebrate It!

The Bottom Image Breaks
all the proportions, but still says
"HEY! I'm A Rooster"

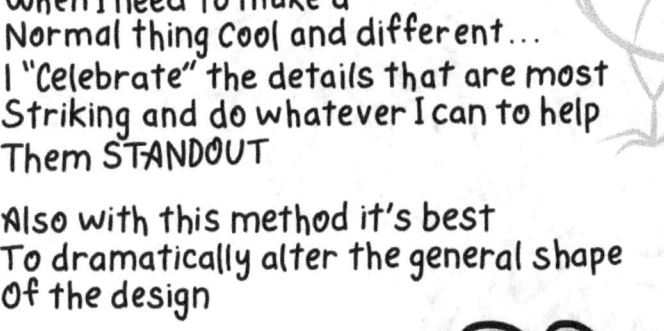

When I need to make a
Normal thing Cool and different...
I "Celebrate" the details that are most
Striking and do whatever I can to help
Them STANDOUT

Also with this method it's best
To dramatically alter the general shape
Of the design

My rooster here
Is taller and built
With more strut
And attitude!

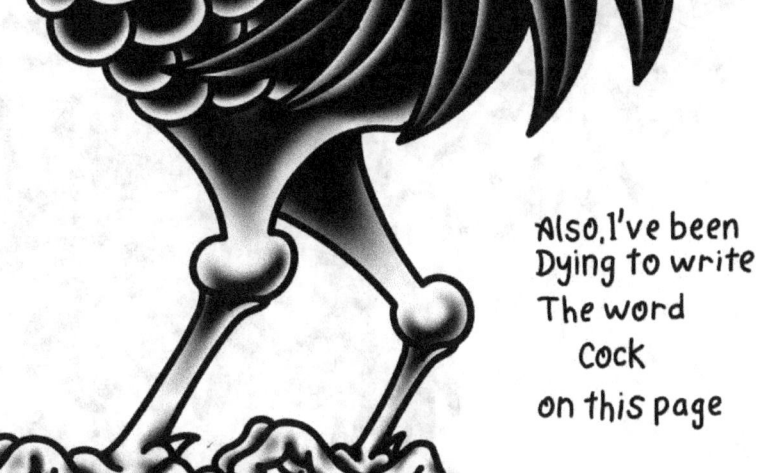

Also, I've been
Dying to write
The word
    Cock
on this page

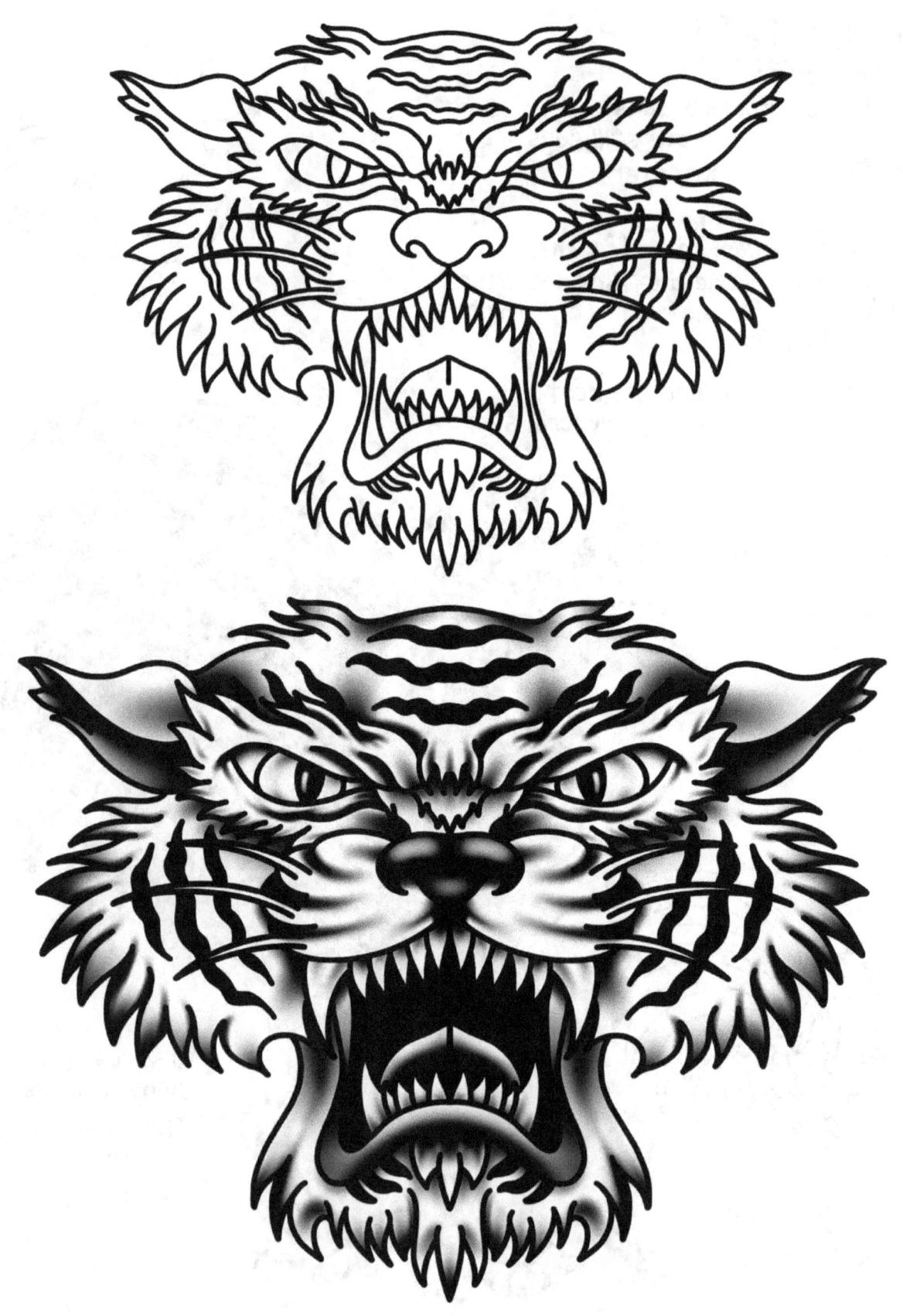

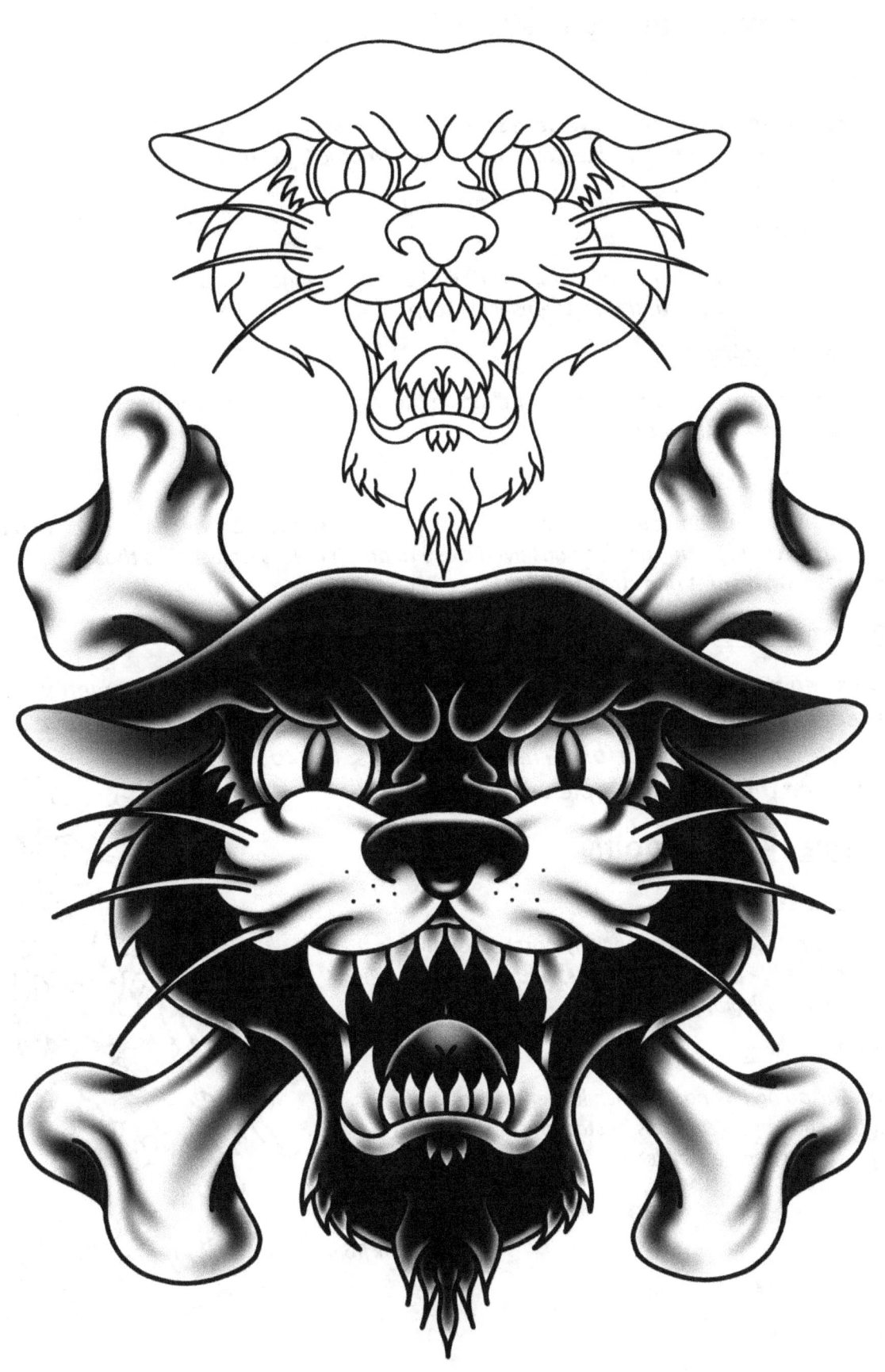

If somebody has an Owl Tattoo, it could mean:

Wisdom & Knowledge:

A very classic association. Owls have been seen for thousands of years (especially in Greek mythology, Ex: Athena had "The little owl" or "Athene Noctua") as the symbol of wisdom, intelligence, and learning.

Mystery & Secrets:

Owls are night creatures, silent hunters. A tattoo of one can suggest that the person is drawn ot mystery, hidden truths, or that they themselves keep things close to the chest.

Protection & Guardianship:

Some cultures saw owls as protectors, watchers in the dark. An owl tattoo might be like carrying a silent guardian, alert, aware, ready.

Life & Death Duality:

In many Native American and ancient beliefs, owls were messengers between the living and the dead. A tattoo could mean someone has lived close to death or loss and carries those experiences with respect and strength.

My Personal Take:

If you see someone with an owl tattoo, you're probably looking at a person who has spent time educating themselves, they don't waste words, and they have a deep sense of what's important. They're watchers, not talkers. They will see things most people will miss.

Historically in tattooing:

Traditional Flash:

Owls show up occasionally, especially perched on a branch. Sometimes they're paired with clocks, hour glasses or skulls. (death – time – wisdom)

Modern Tattooing:

Modern Tattooing has had a much larger adoption of owls. I think they pop up as symbols of staying sharp and seeing through people's bullshit.

Line work from cover >

Absolutely Shameless Self-Promotion

Tattoo Flash Book One — Artwork by: David Lee Lough

Tattoo Flash Book Three — Artwork by: David Lee Lough

Tattoo Flash Book Four — Artwork by: David Lee Lough

Tattoo Flash Book Five — Artwork by: David Lee Lough

Tattoo Flash Book Six — Artwork by: David Lee Lough

Tattoo Flash Book Two — Artwork by: David Lee Lough

Shaded Version of Cover Image

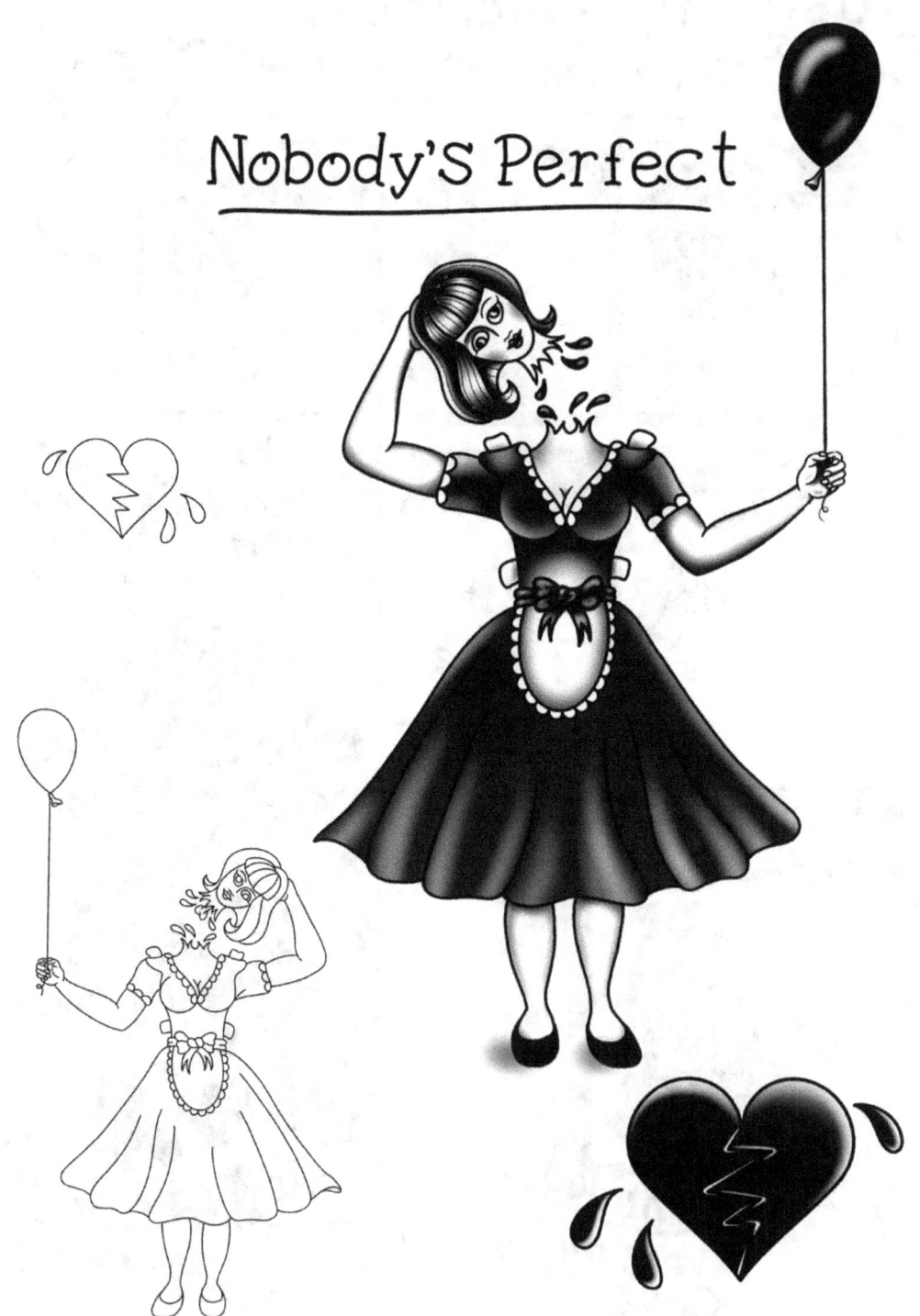

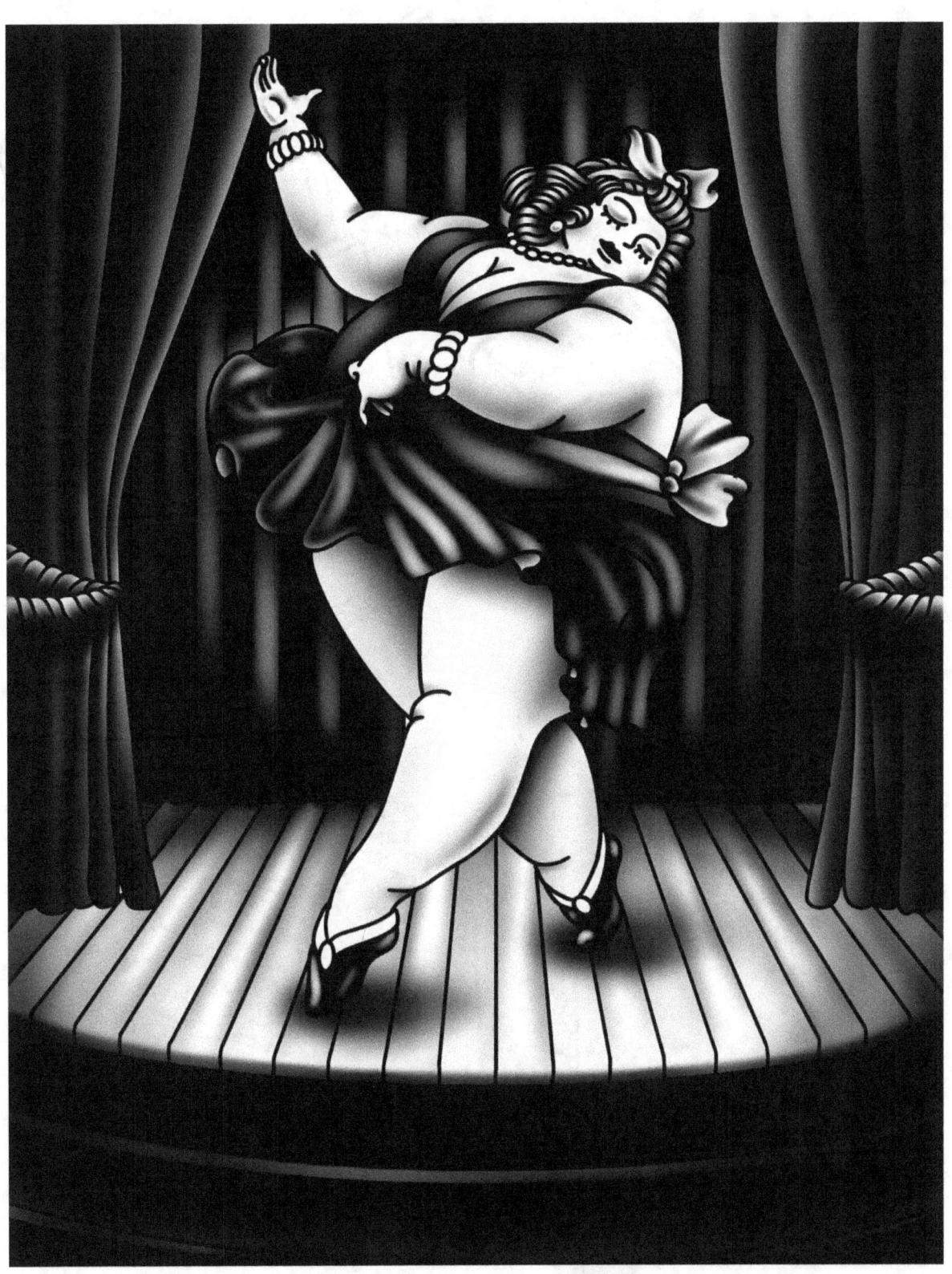

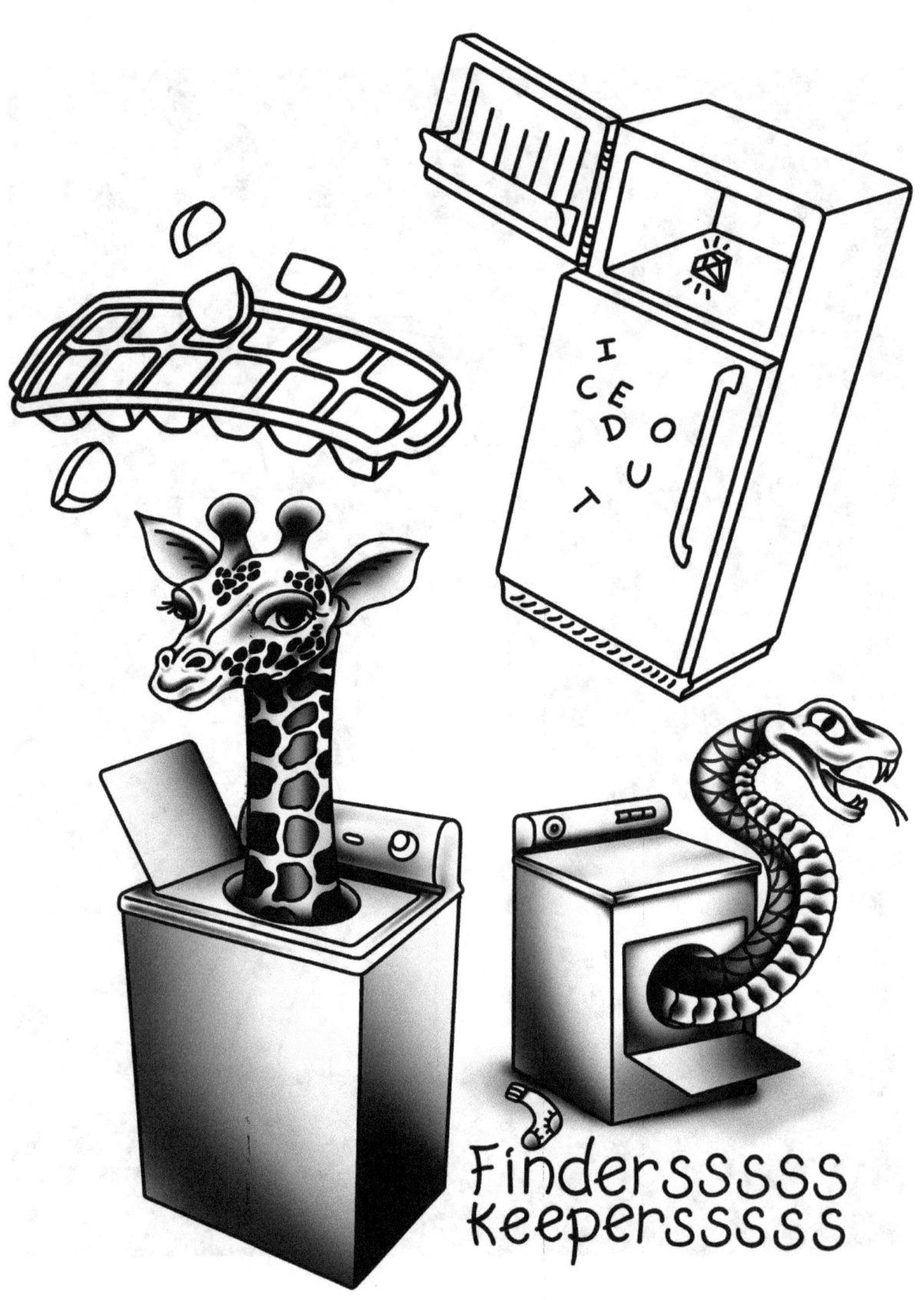

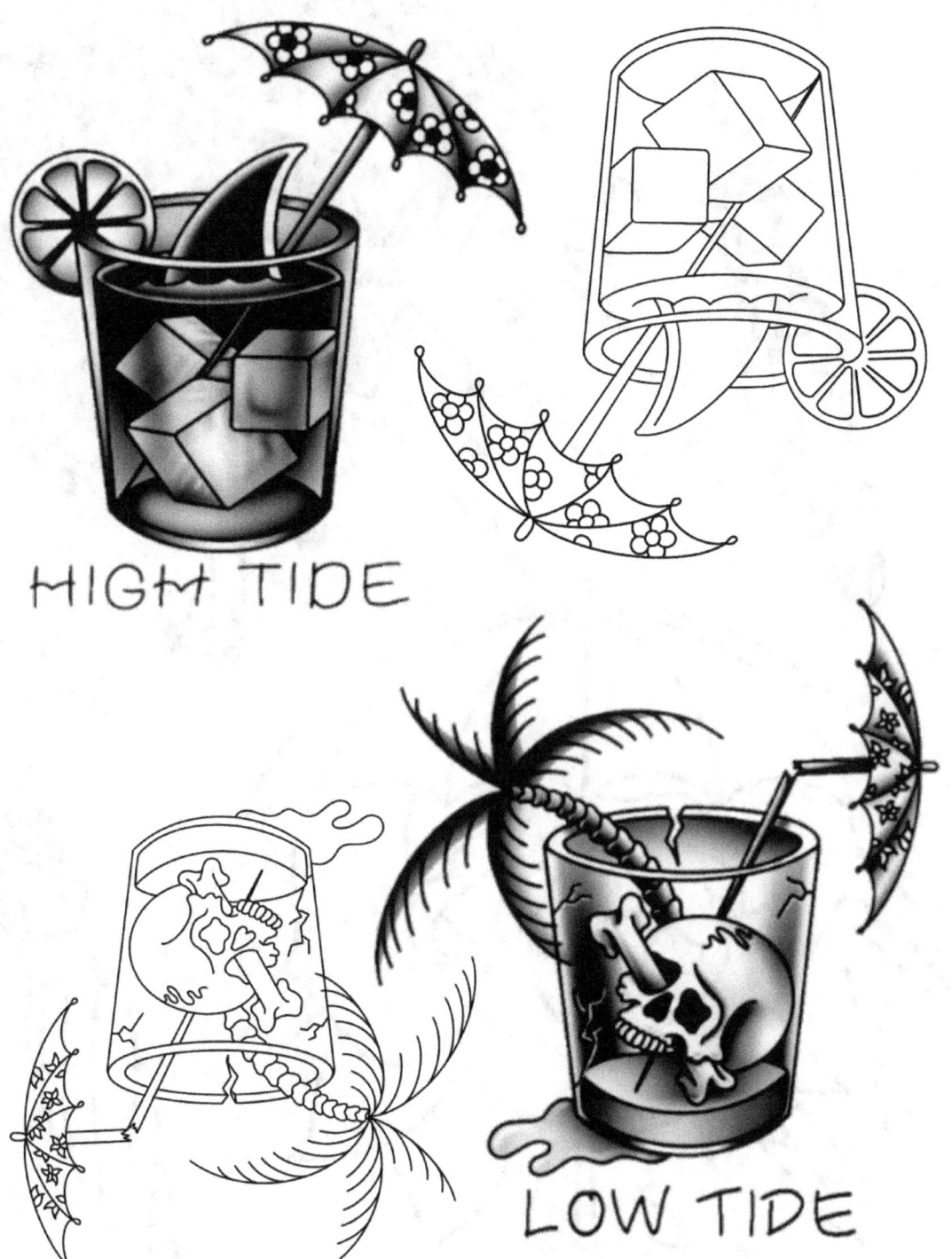

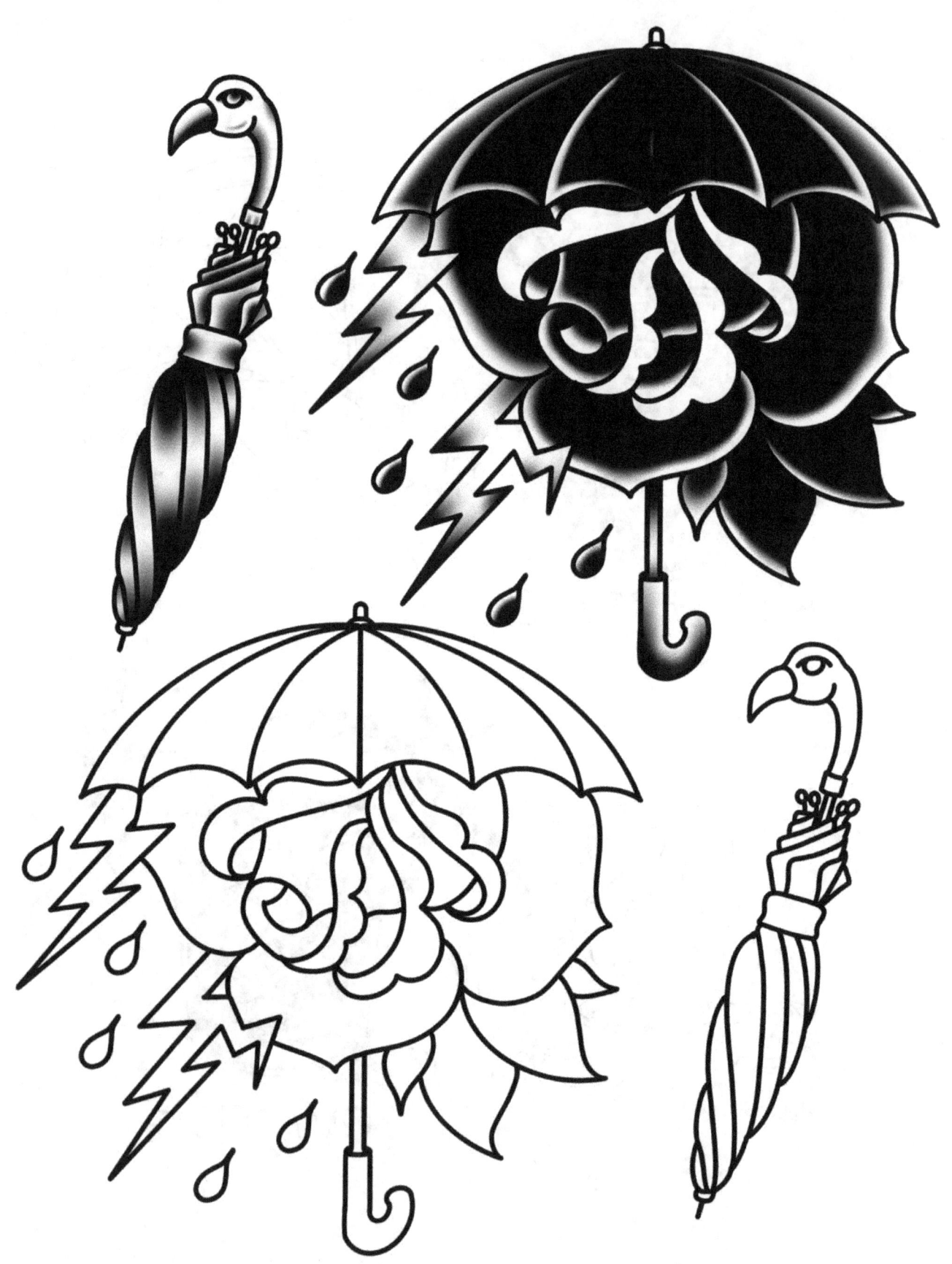

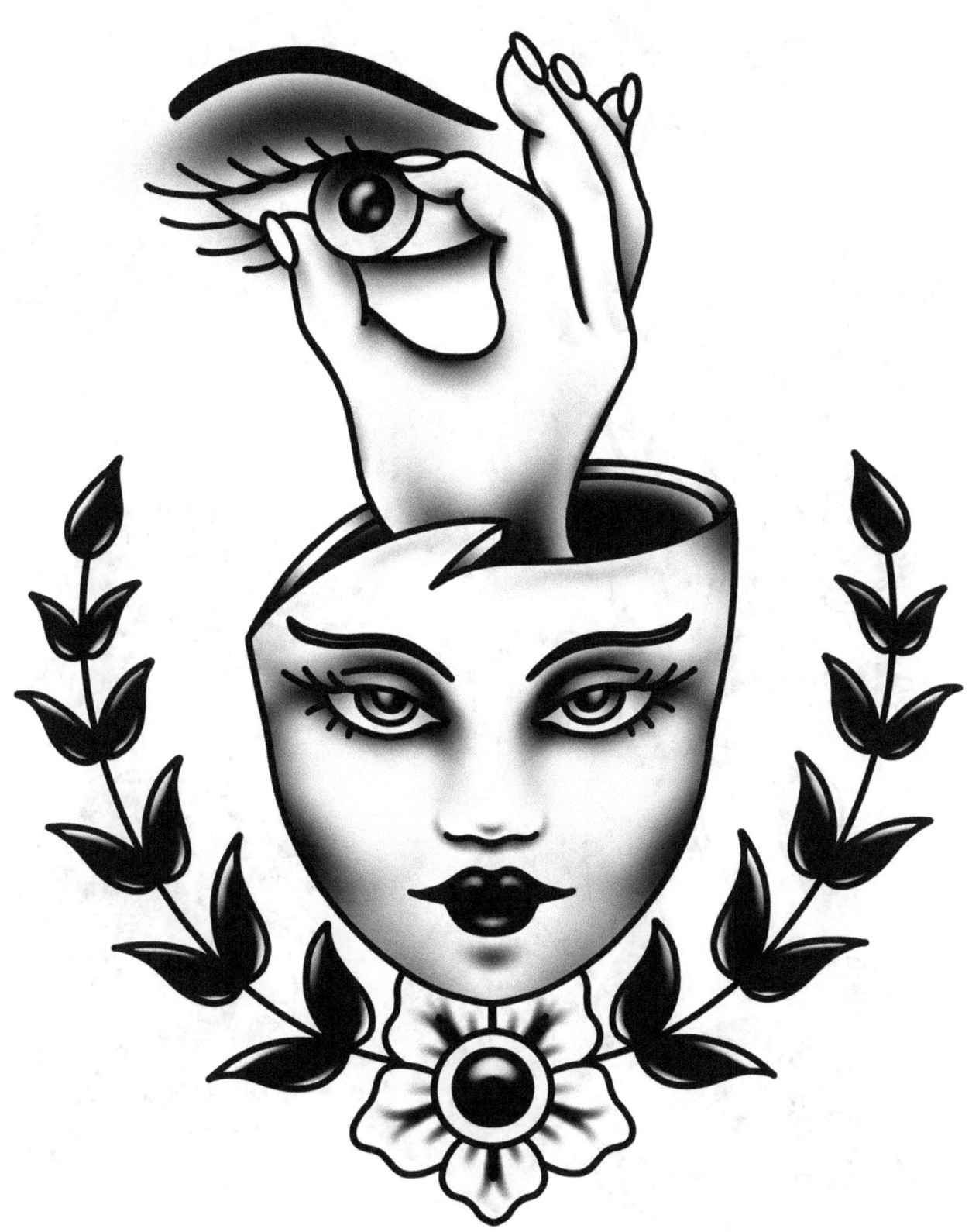

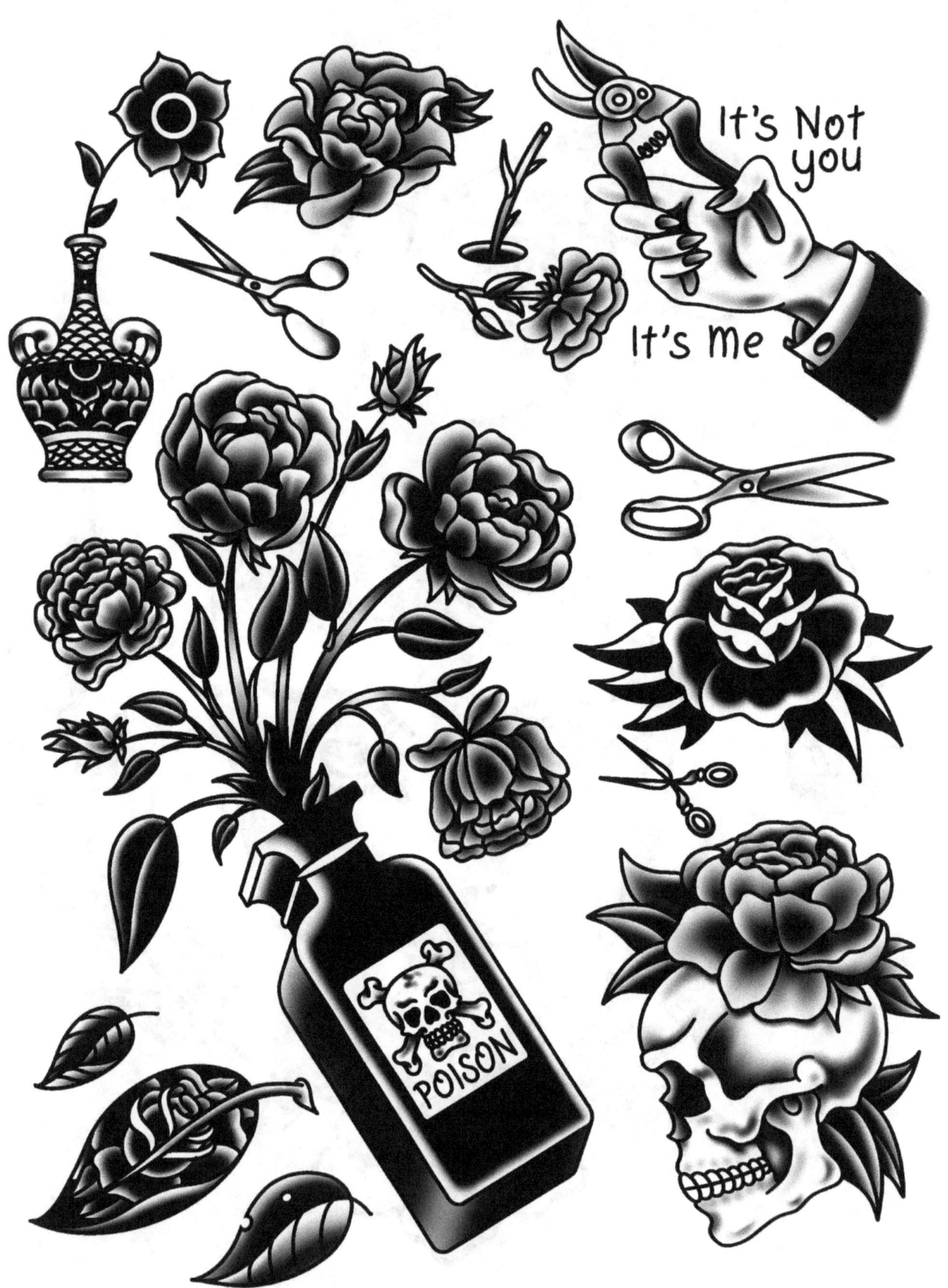

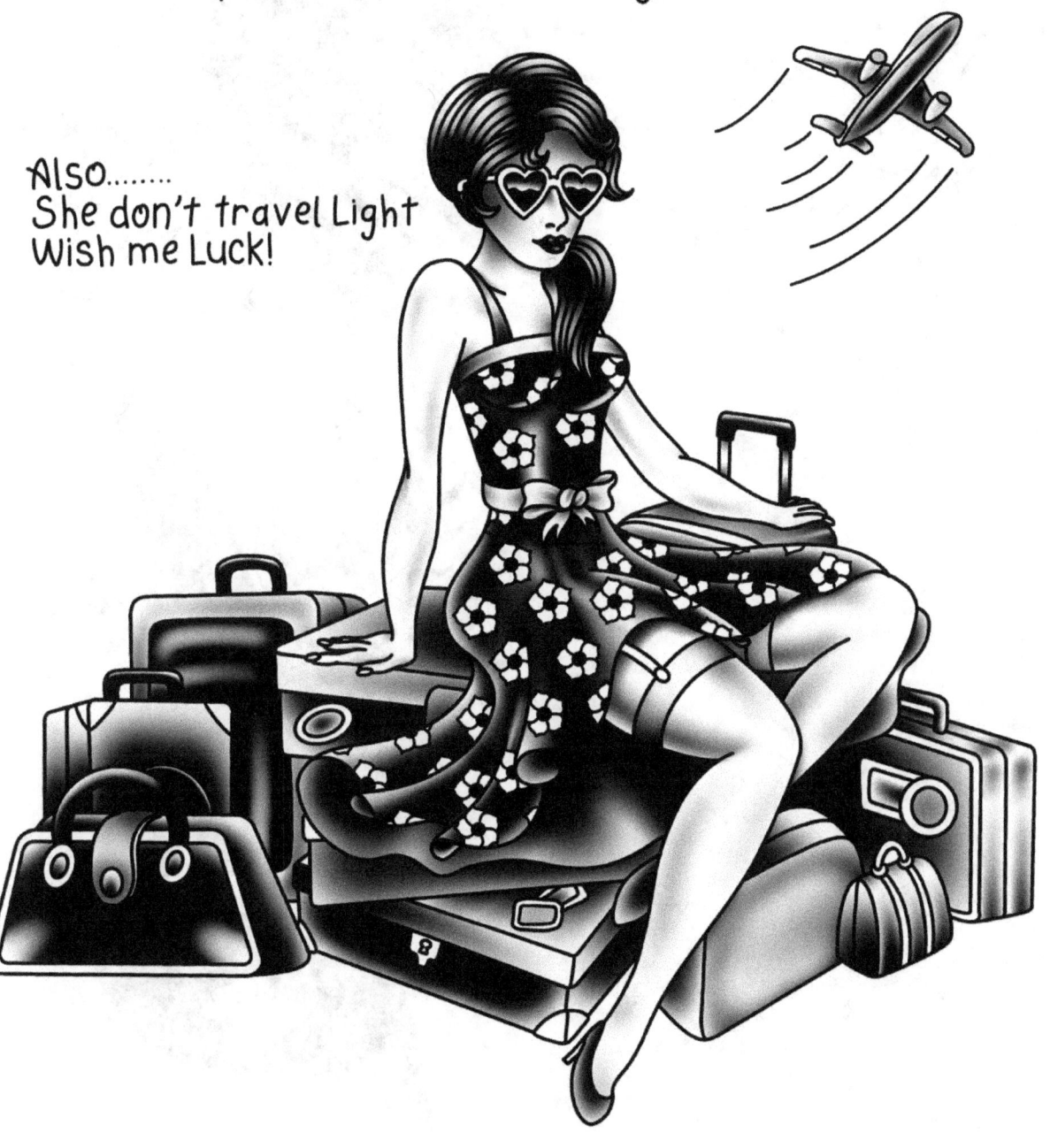

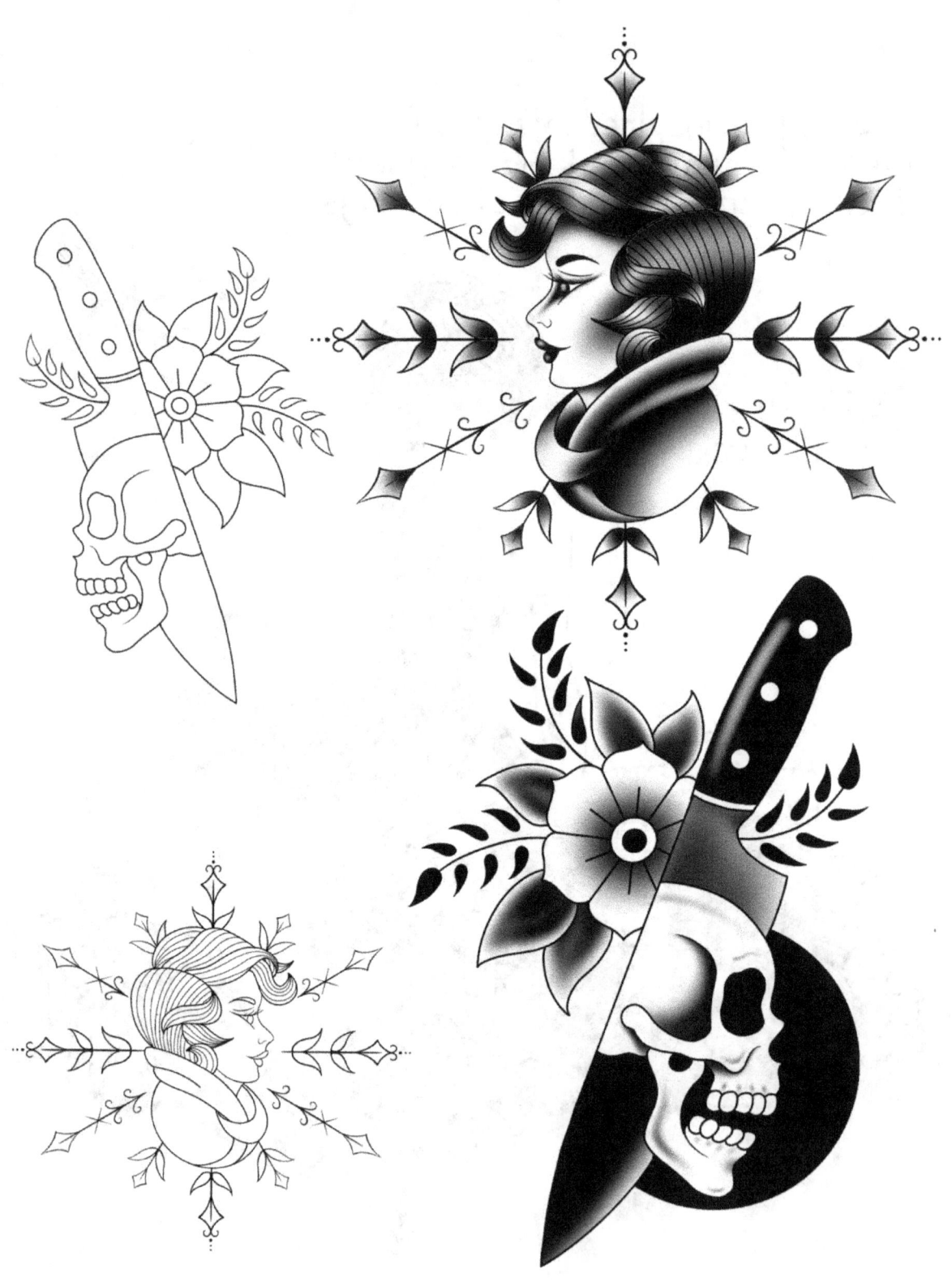

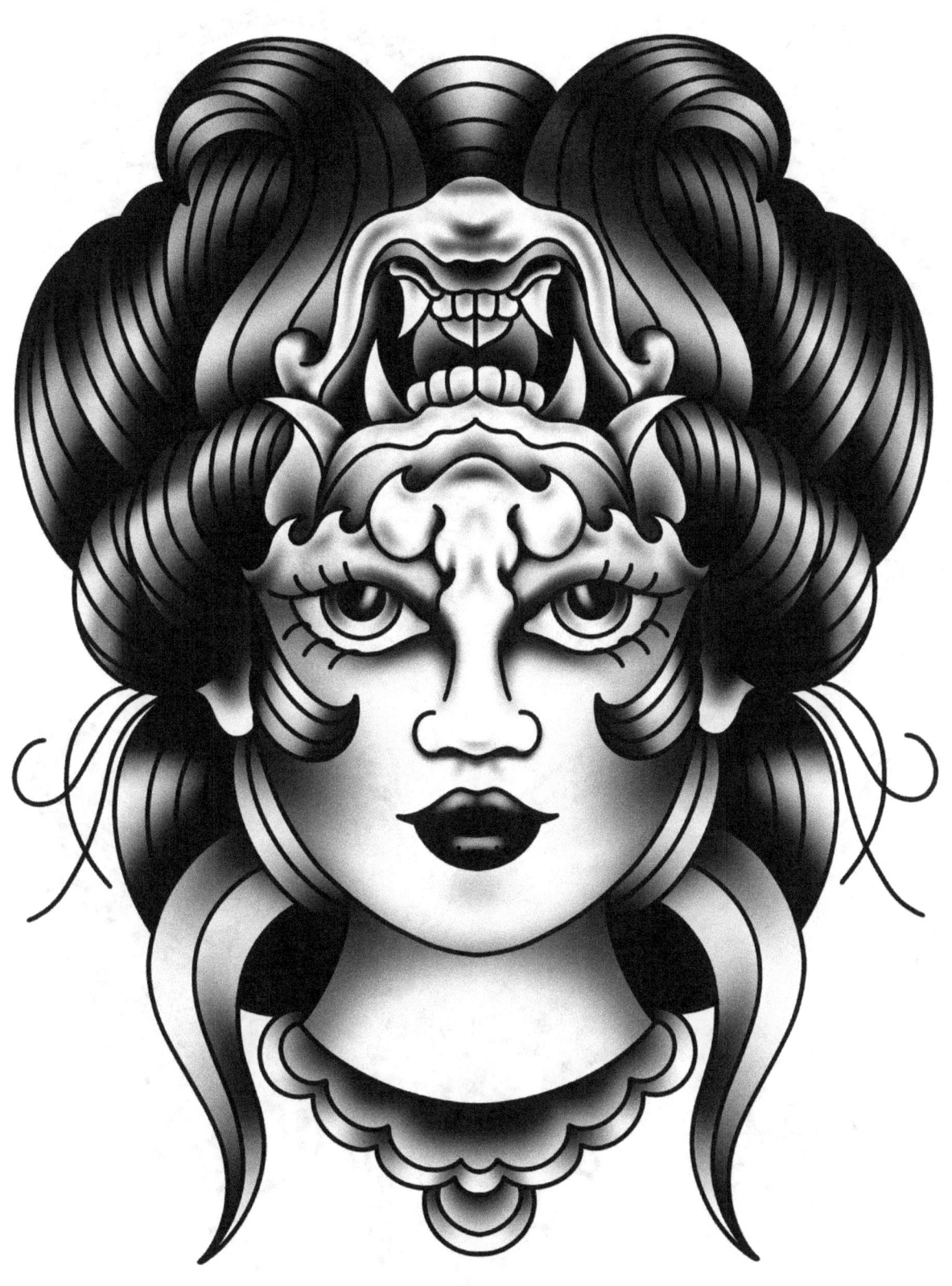

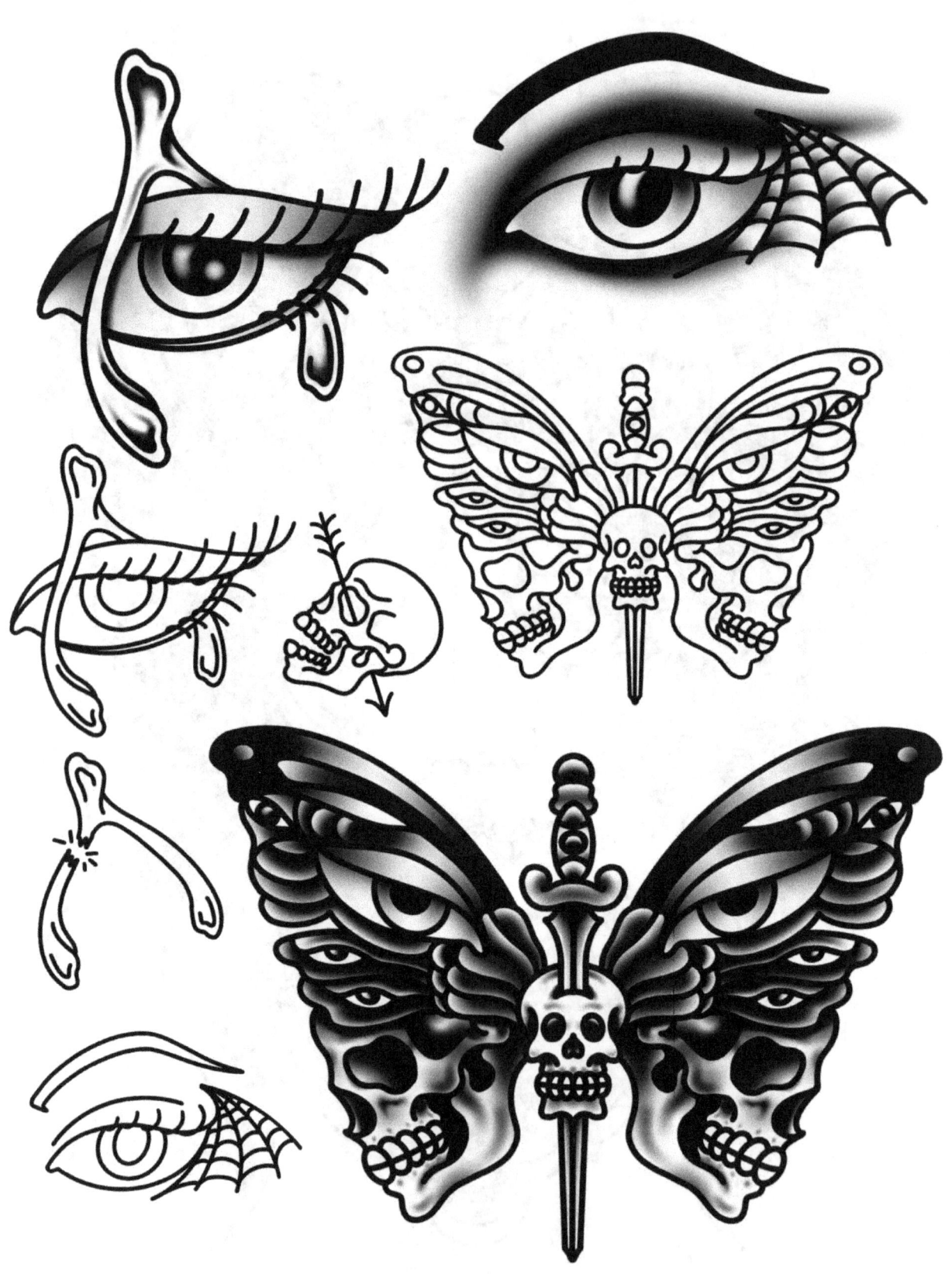

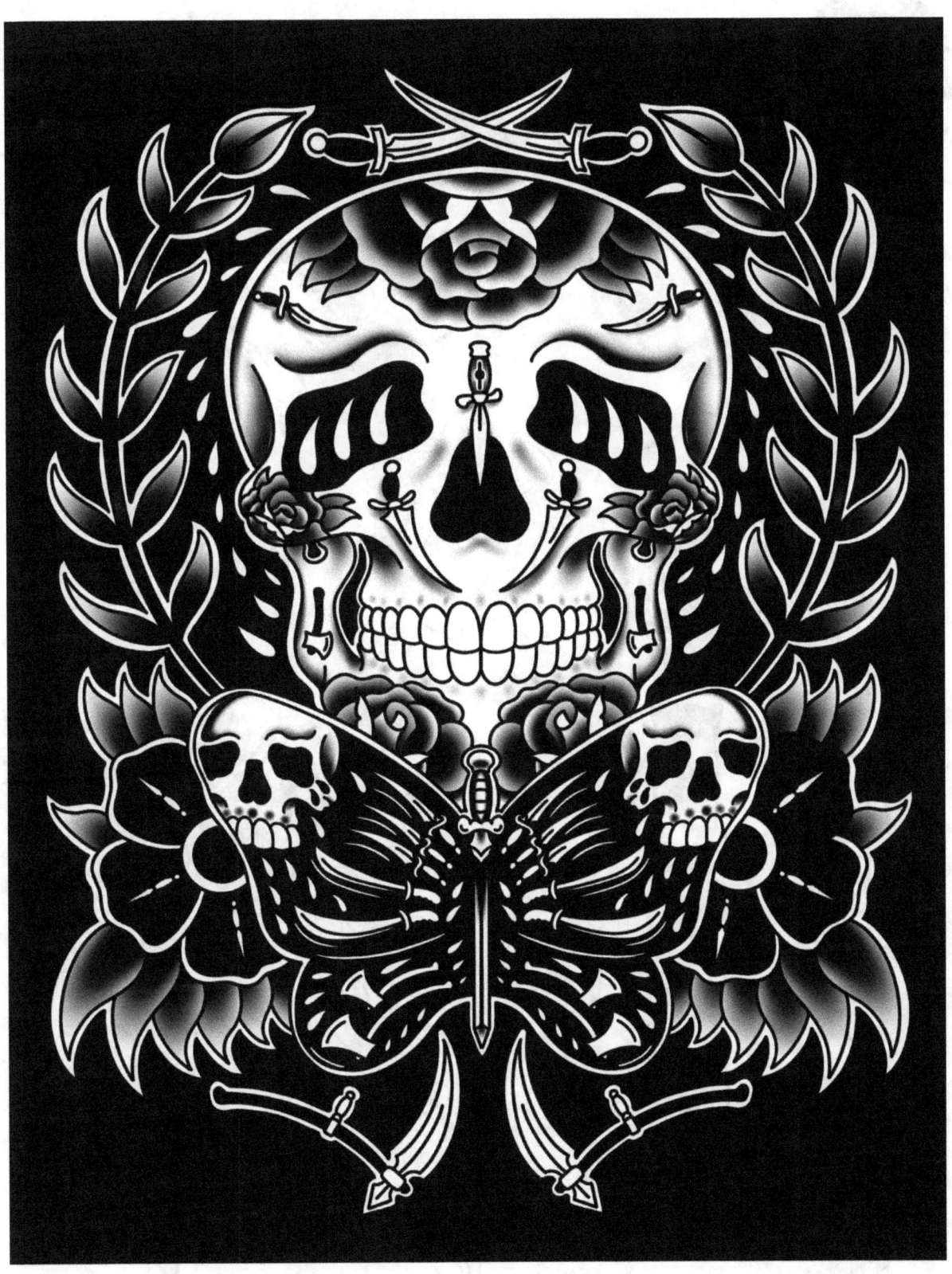

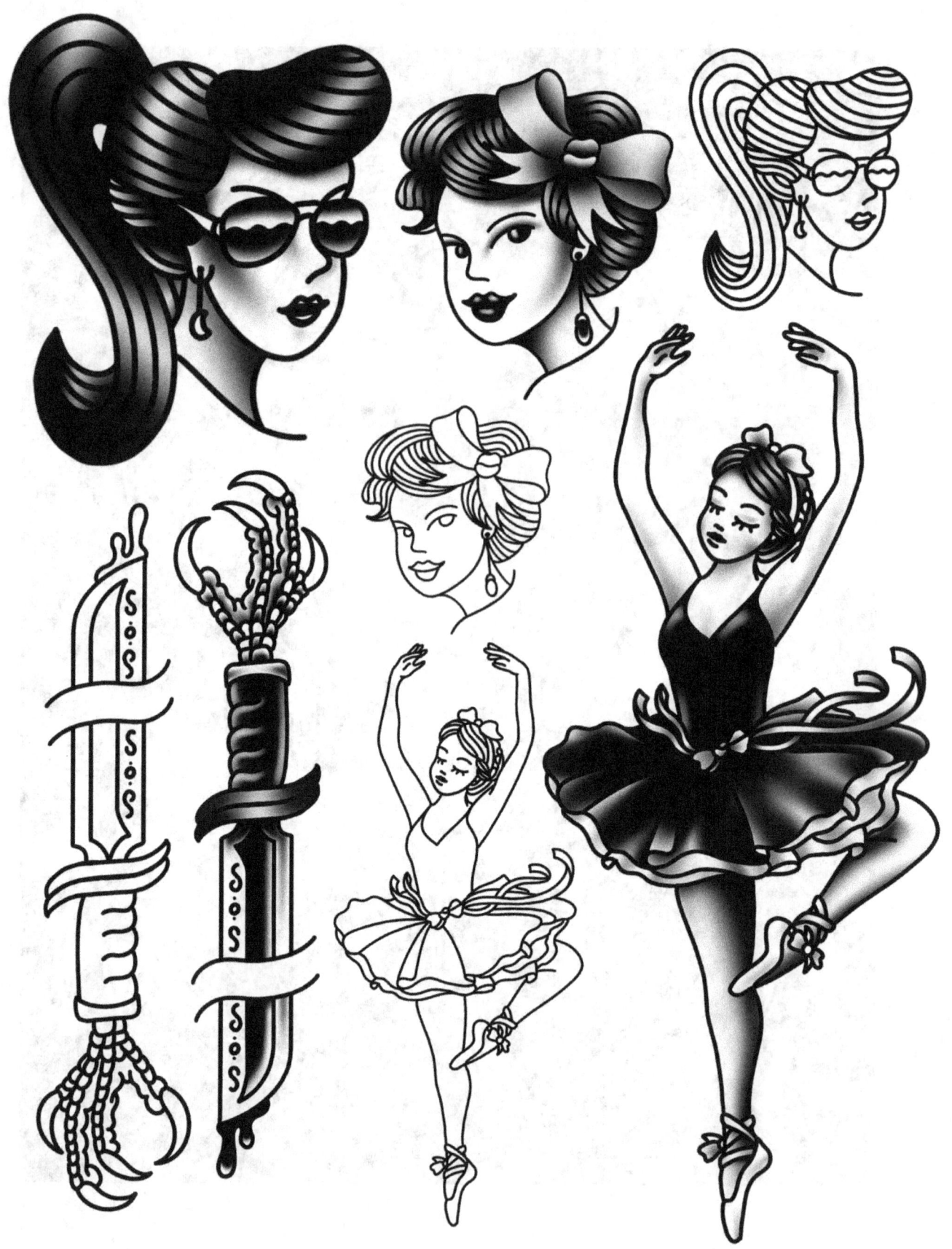

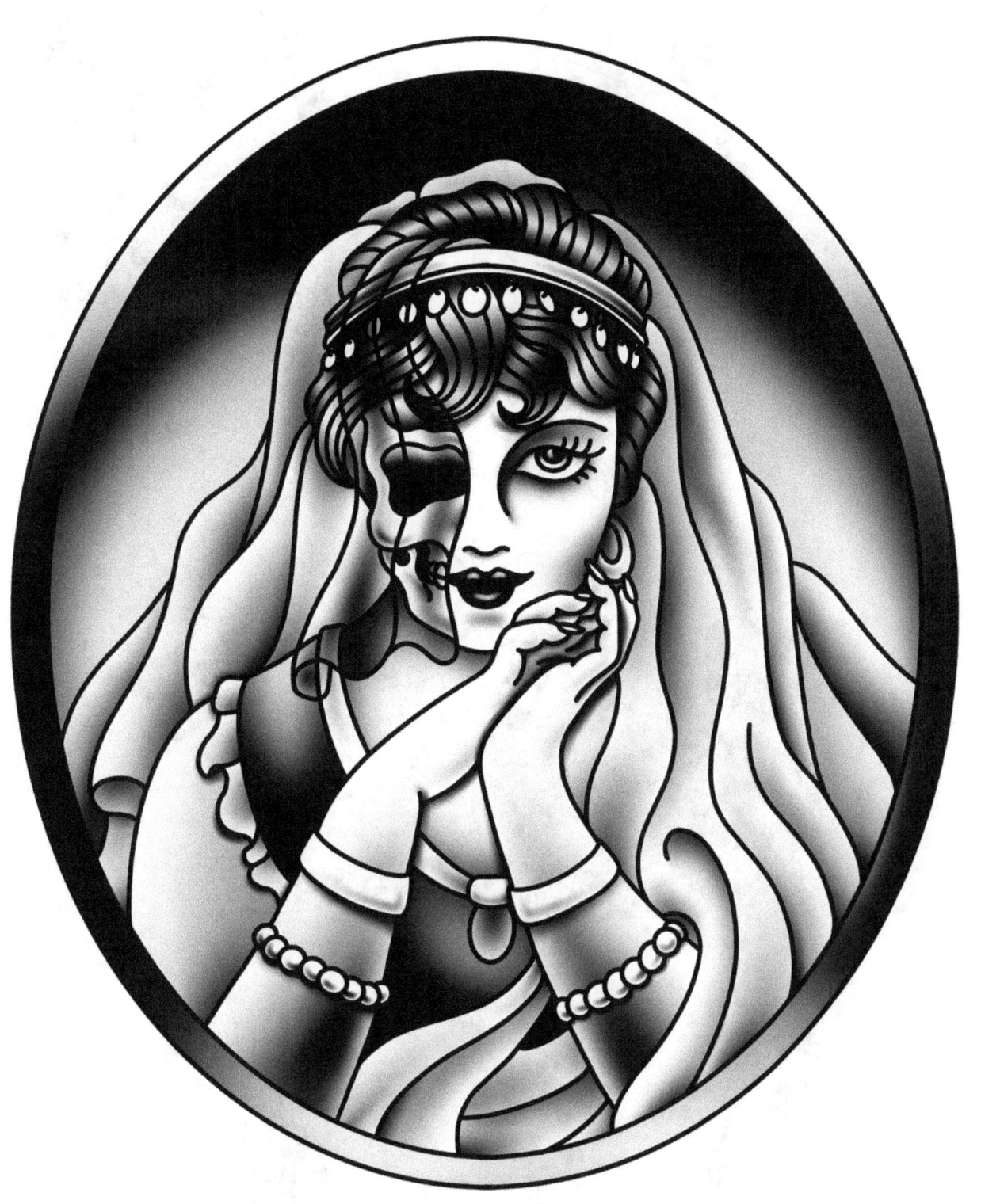

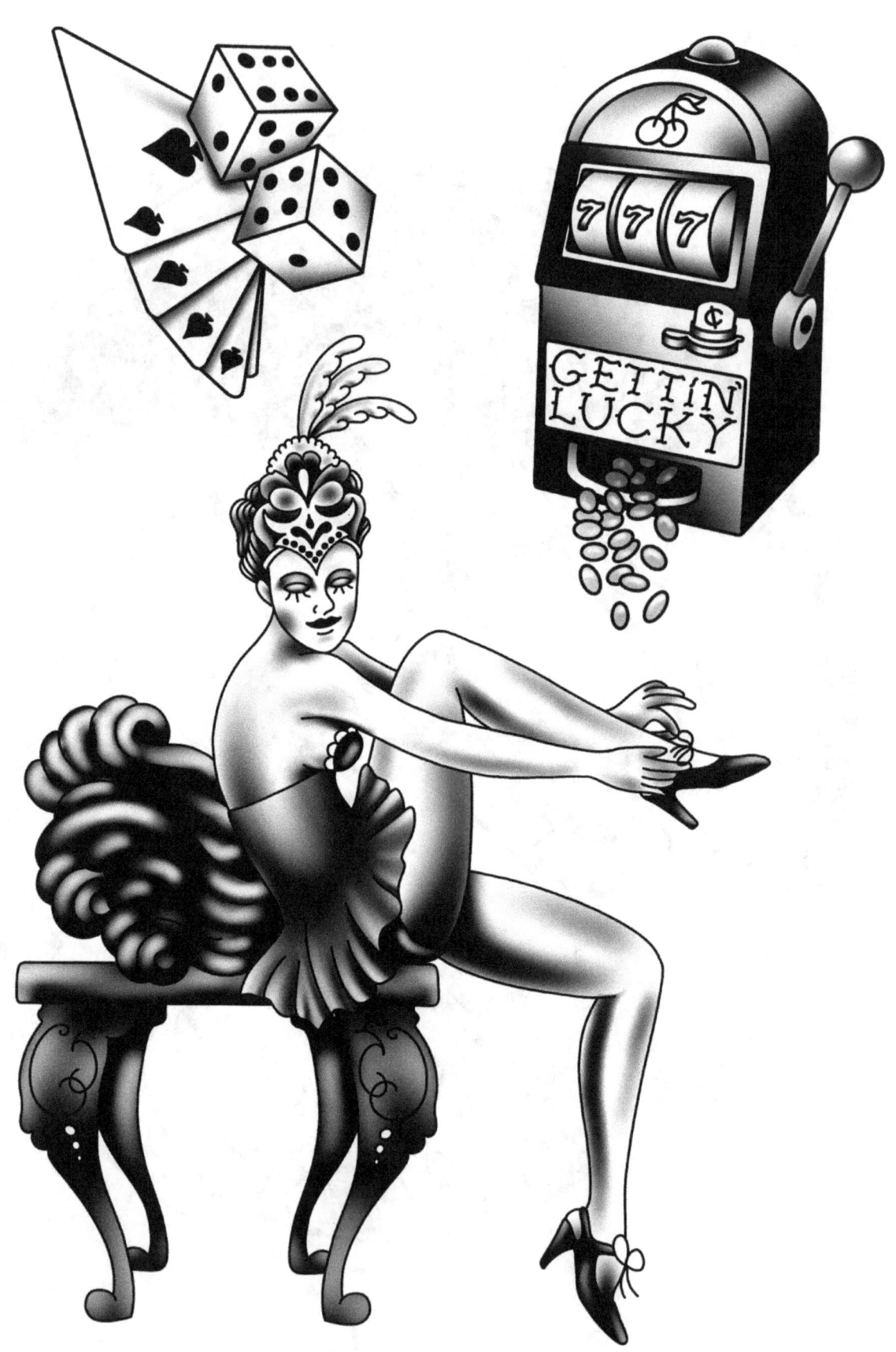

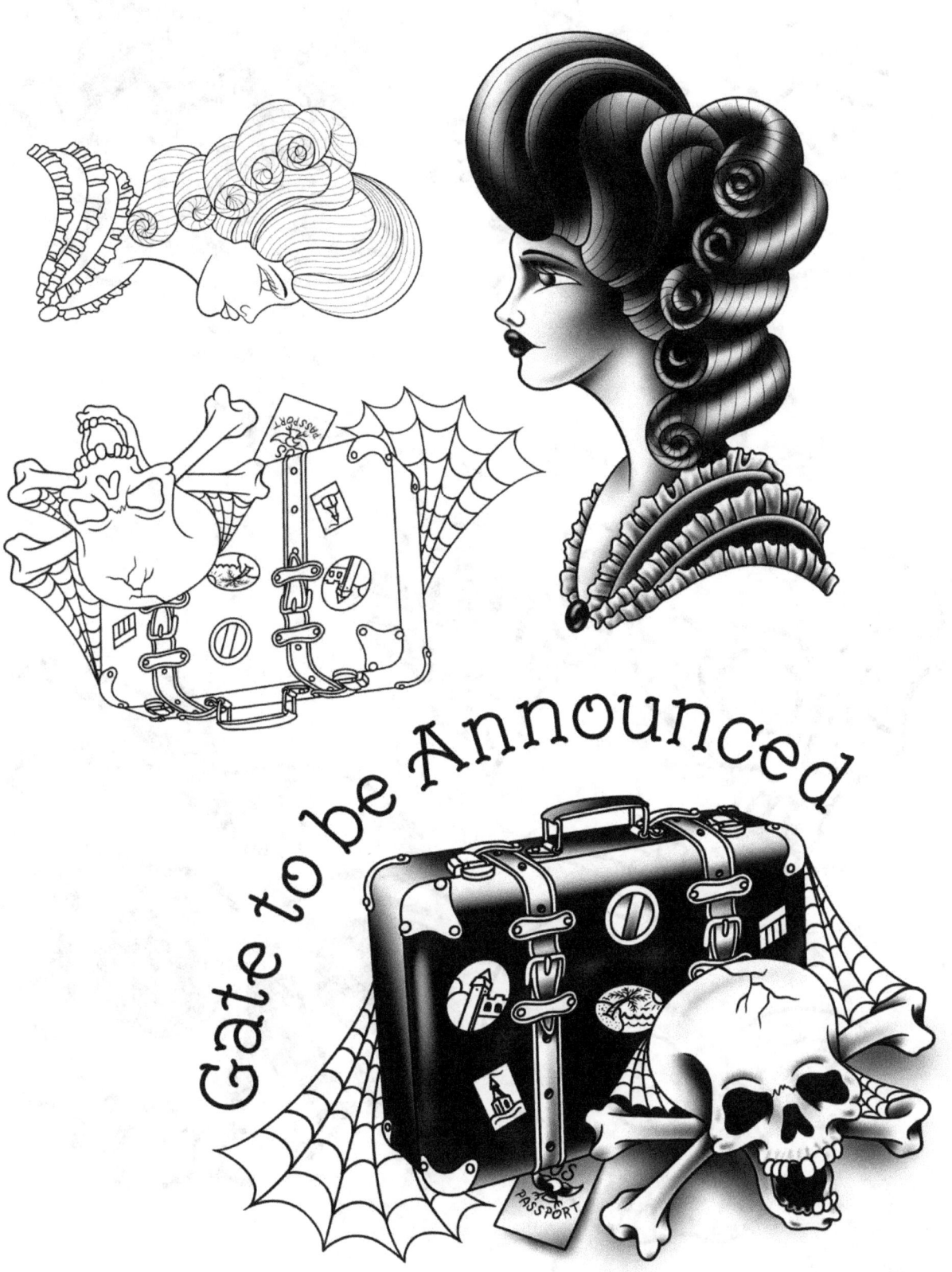

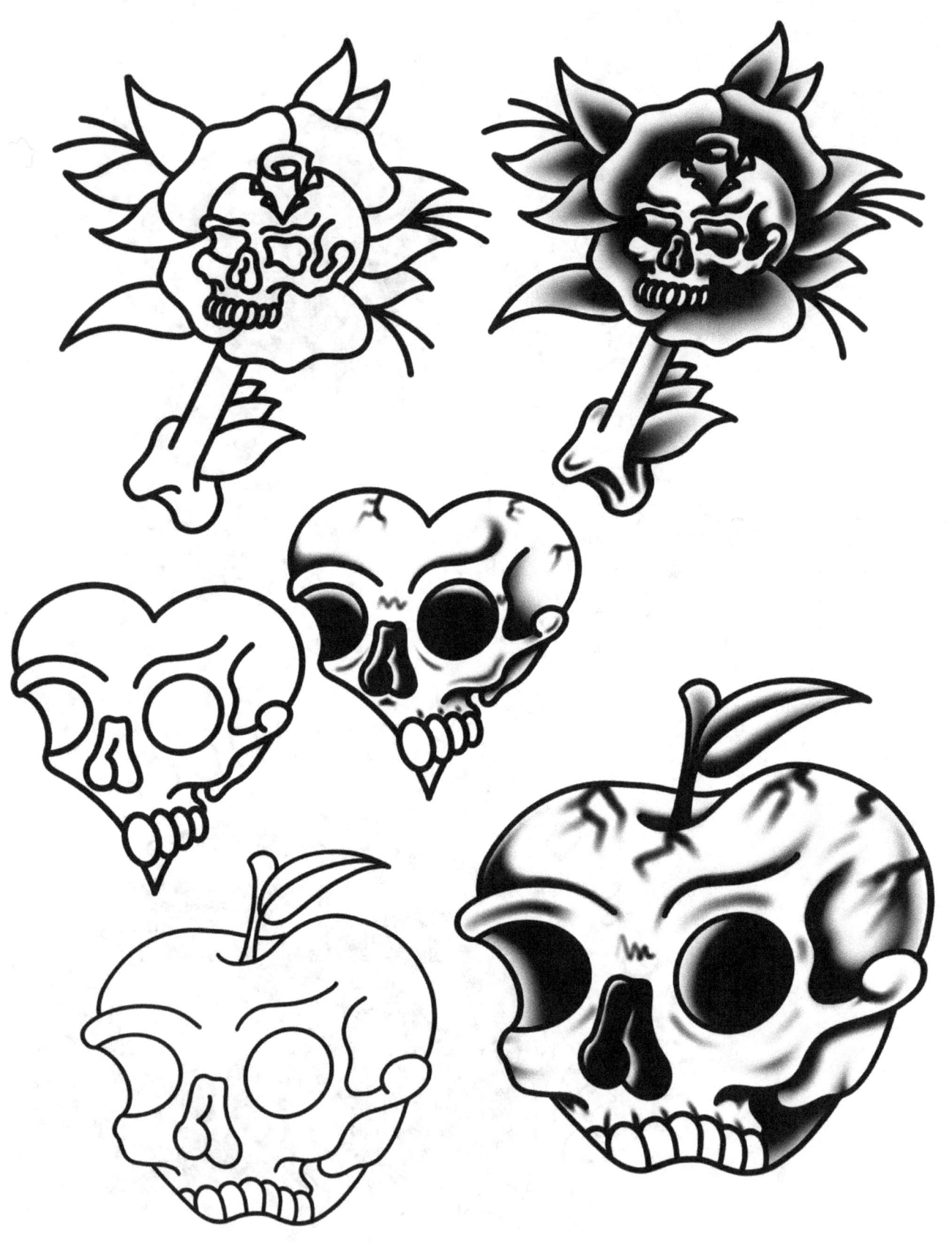

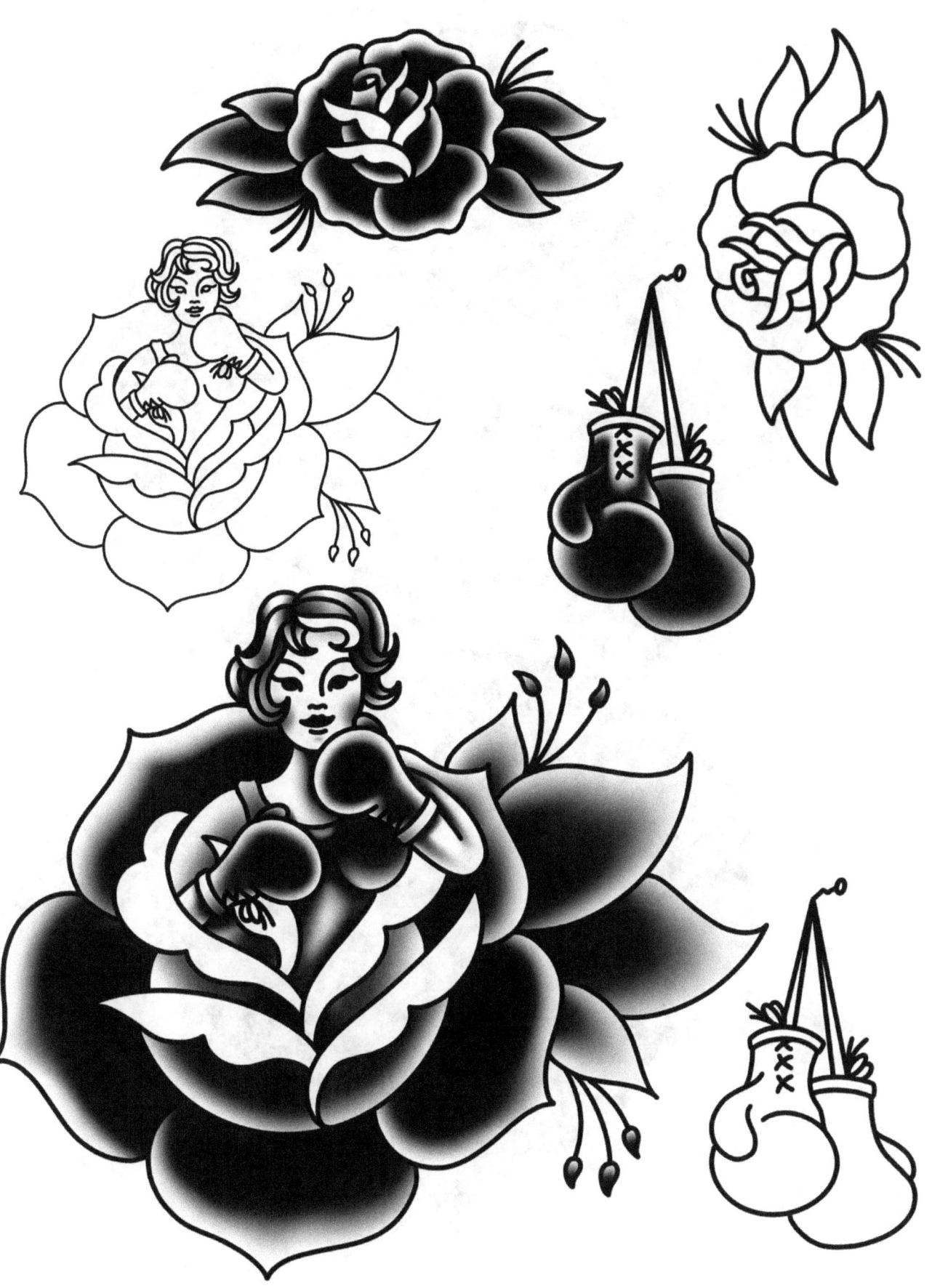

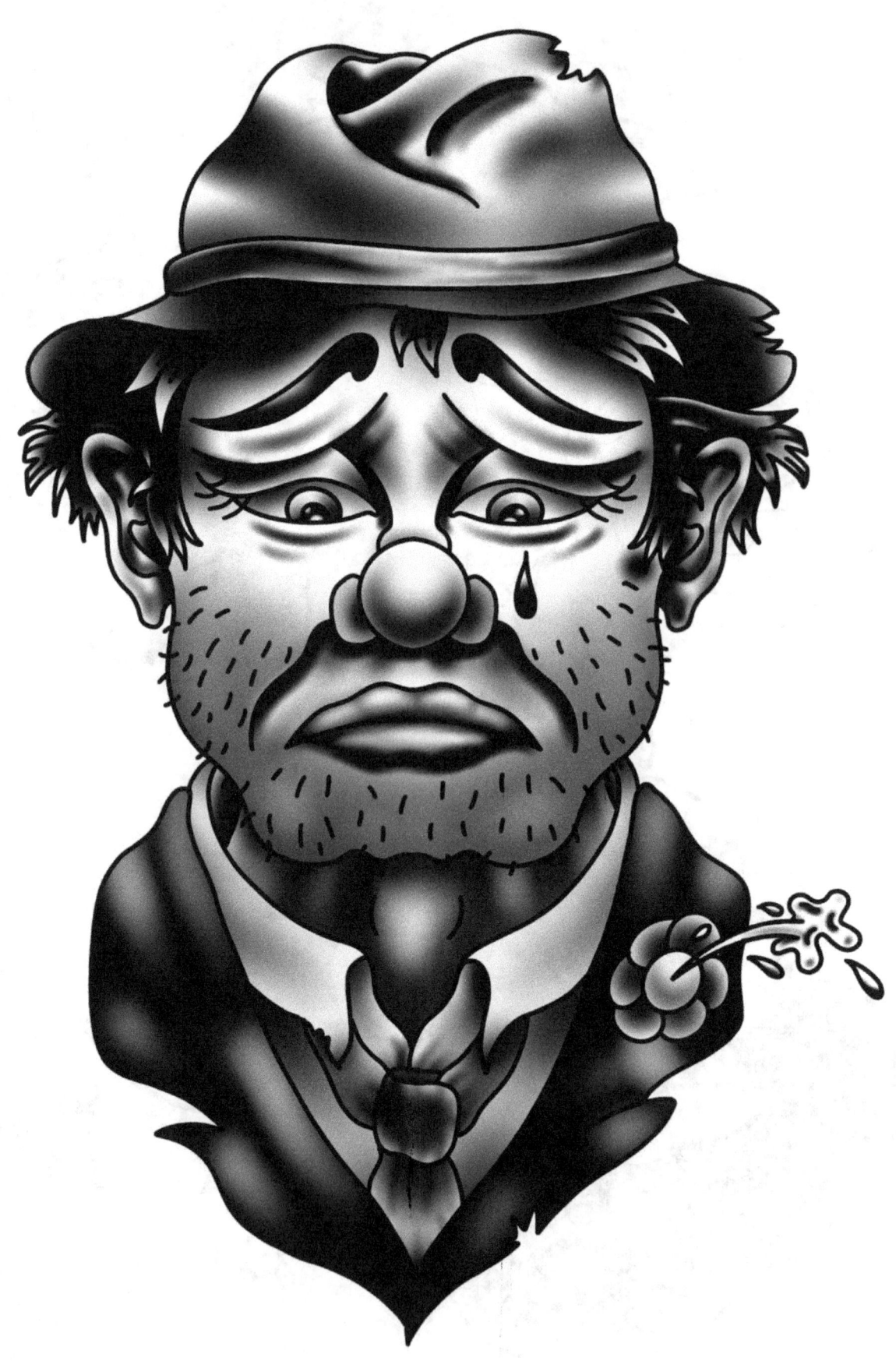

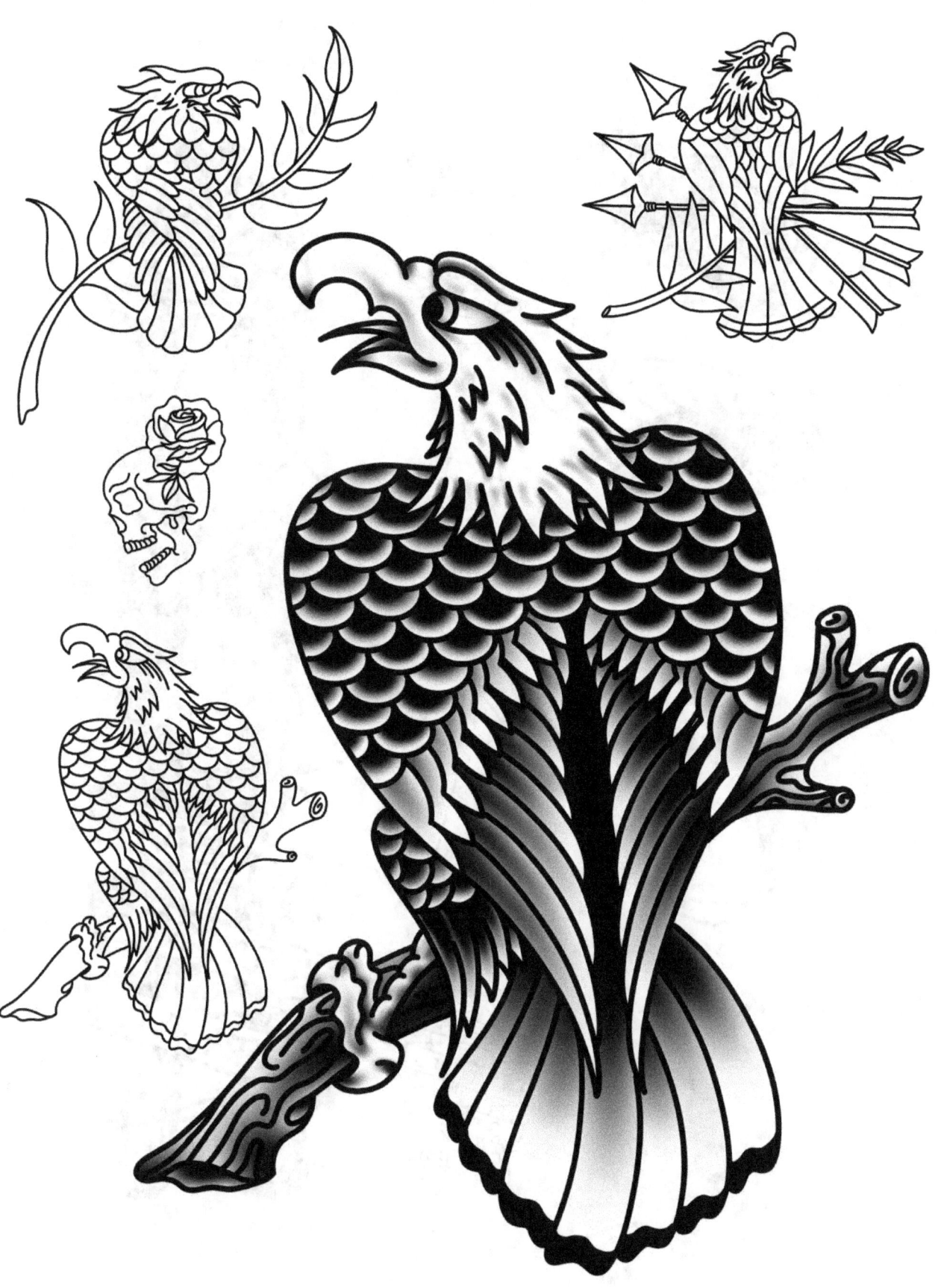

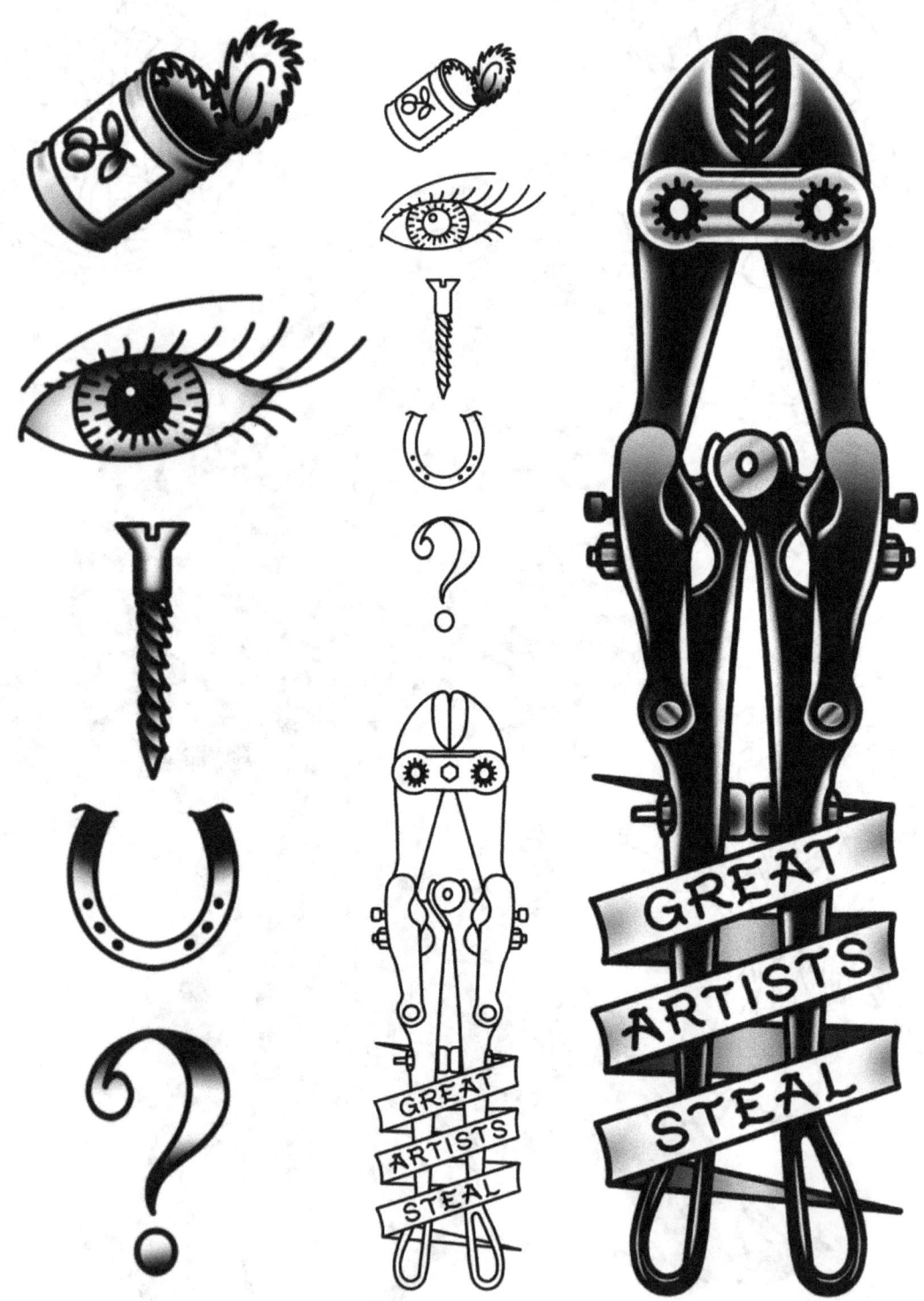

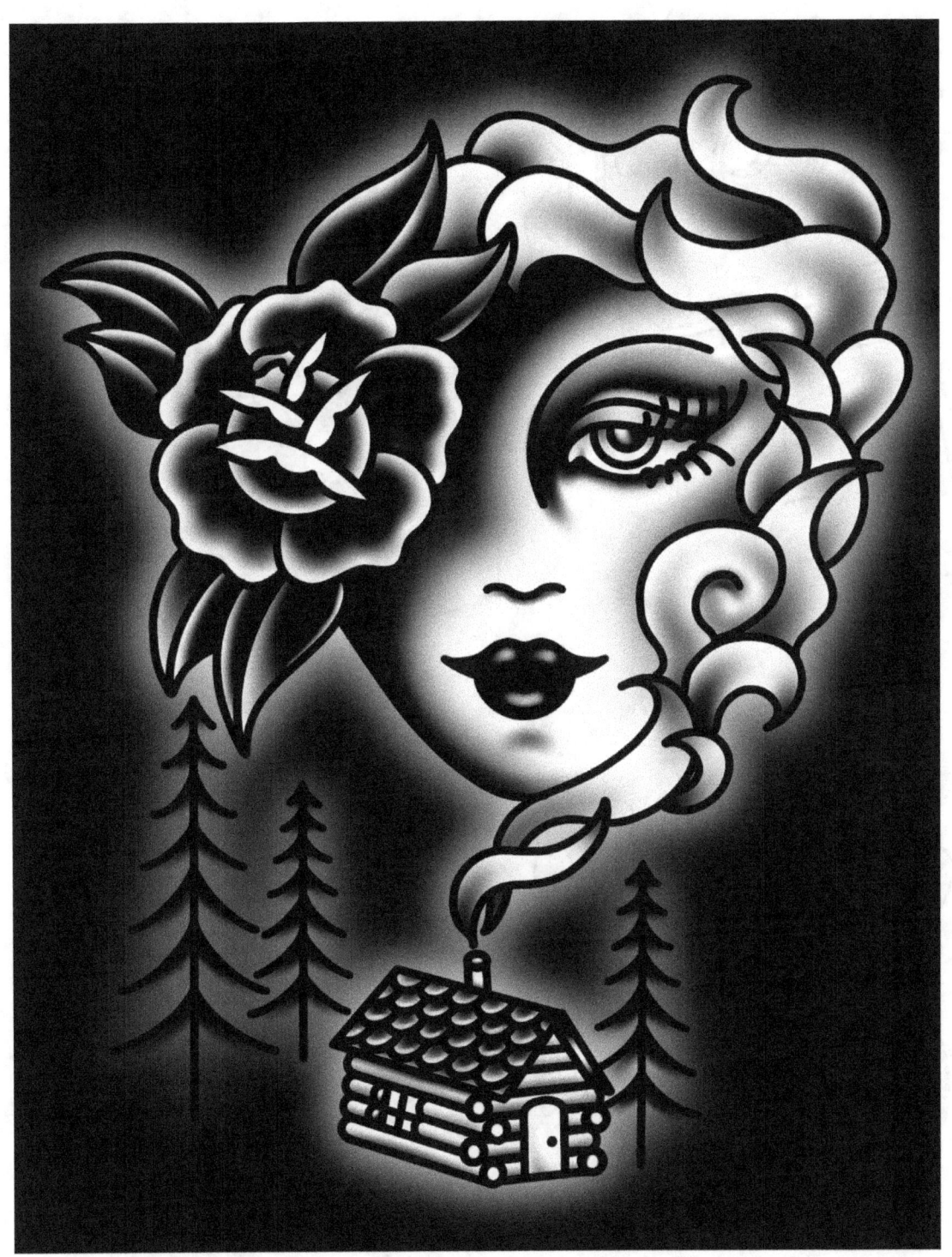

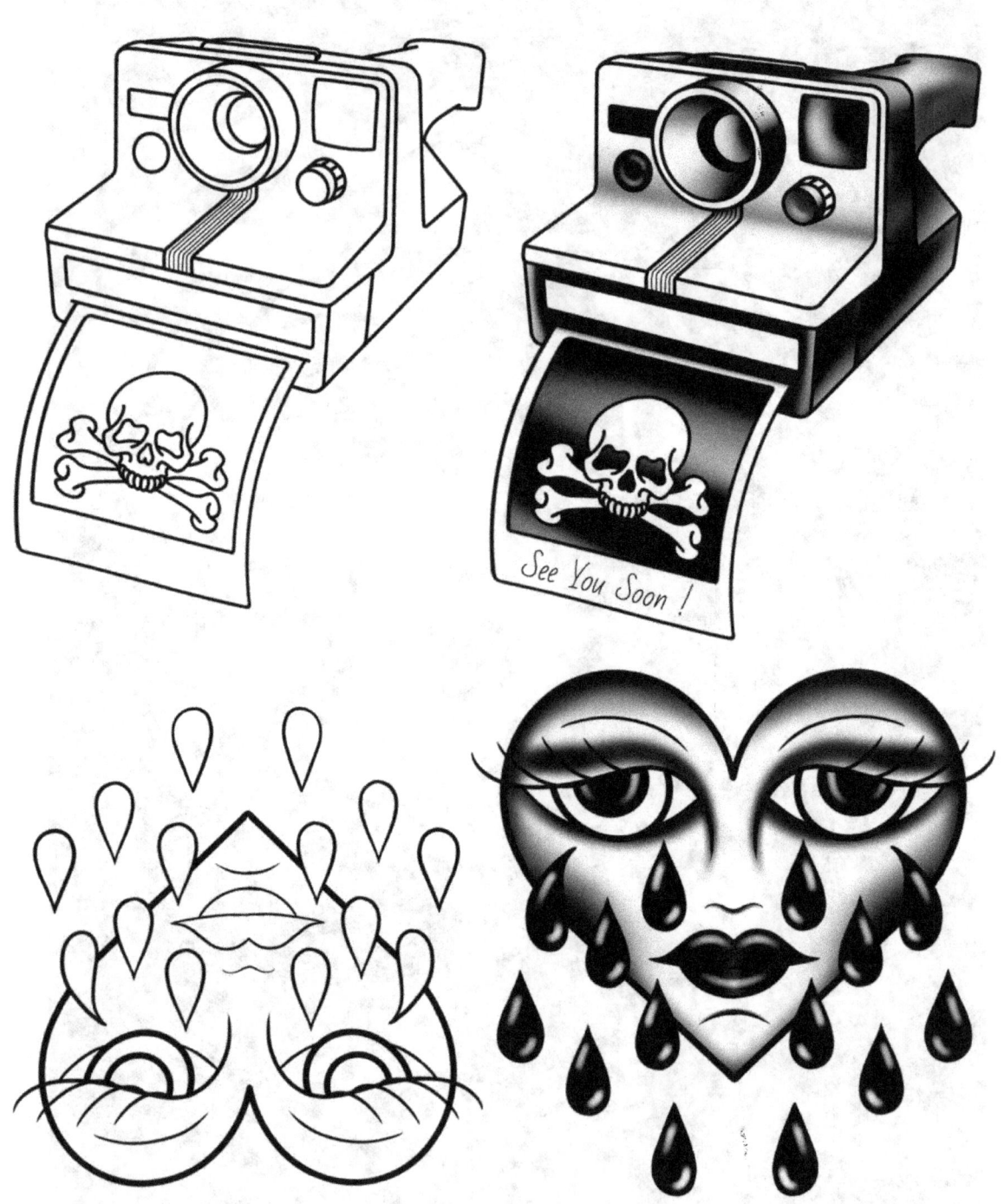

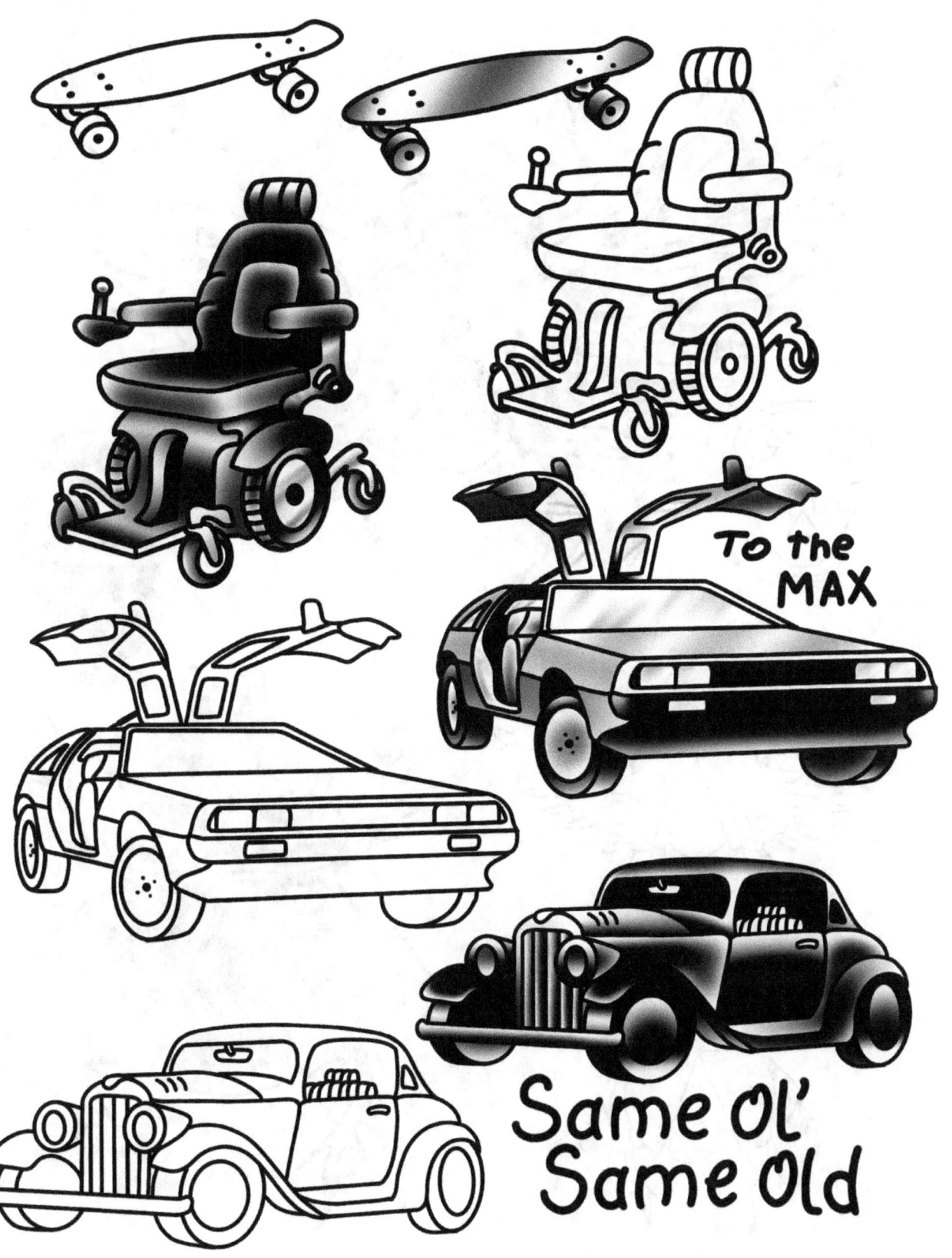

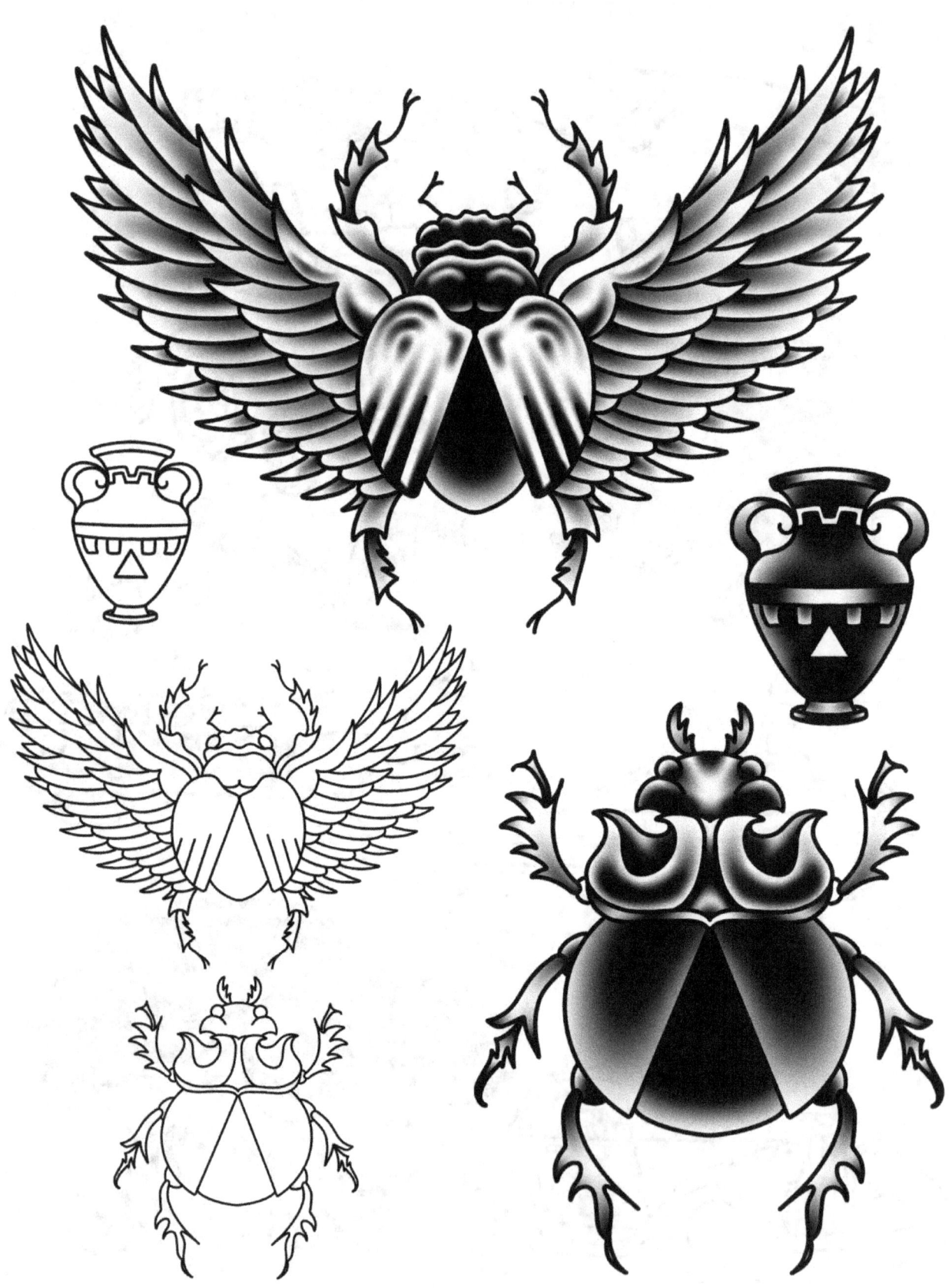

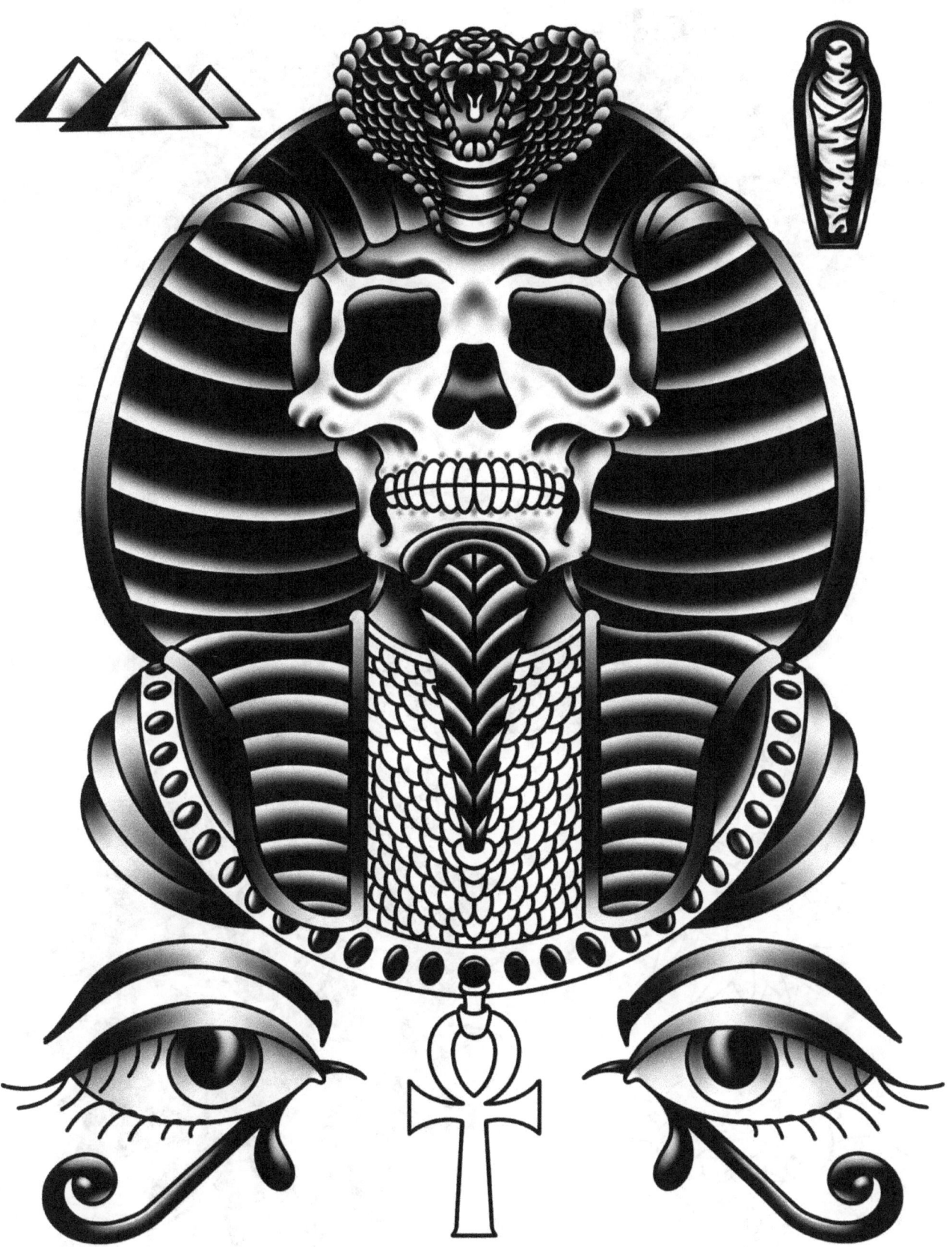

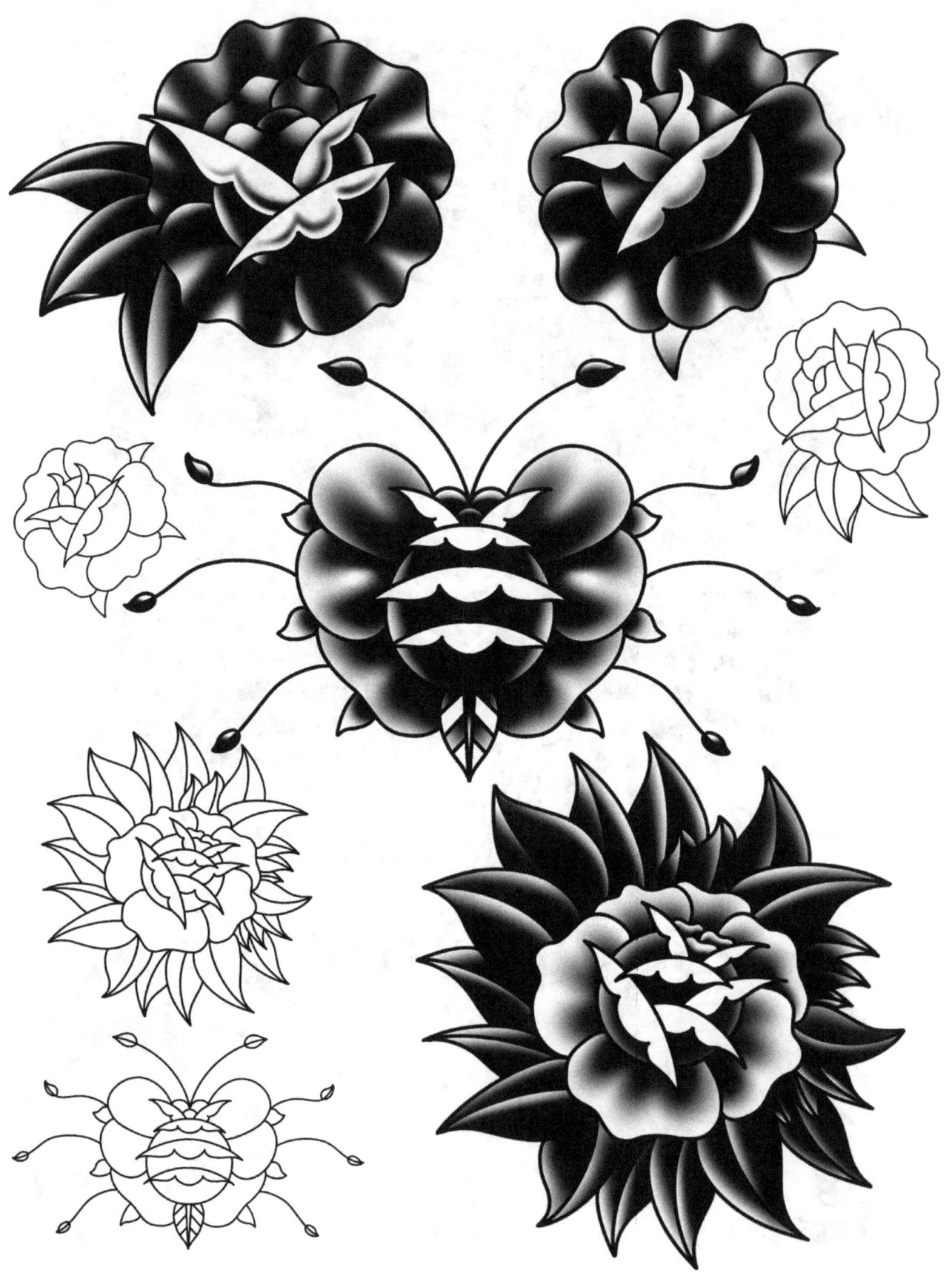

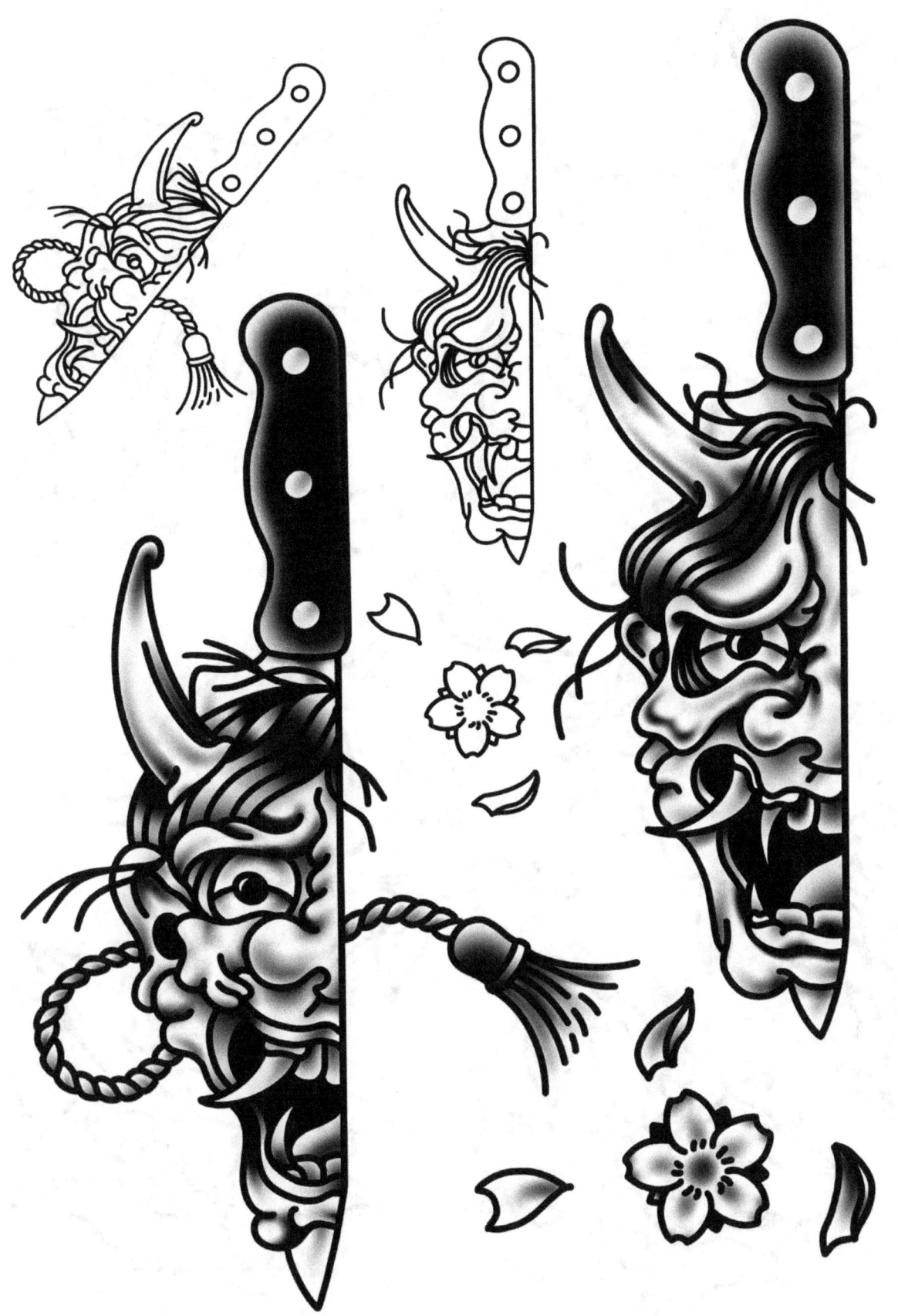

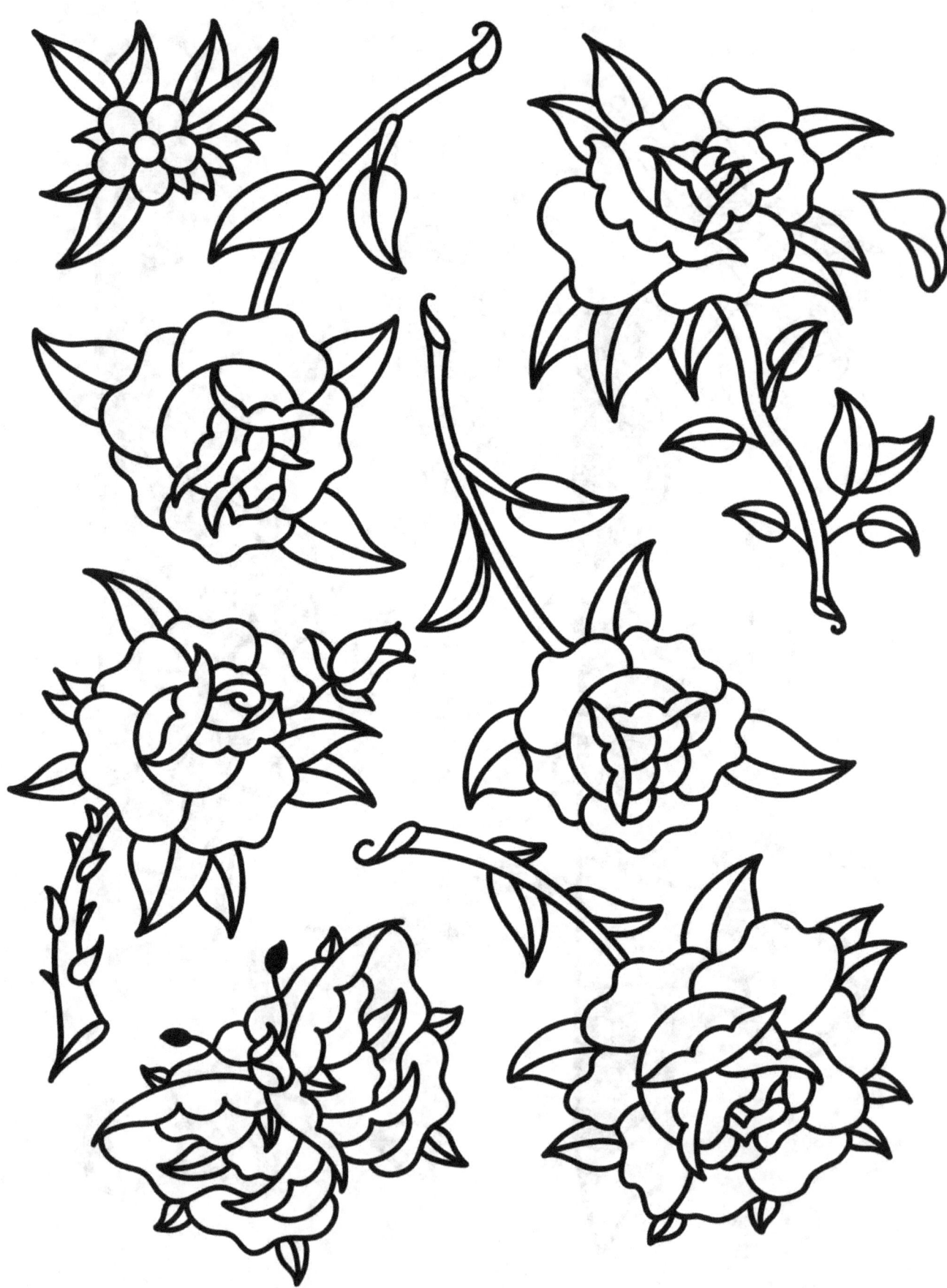

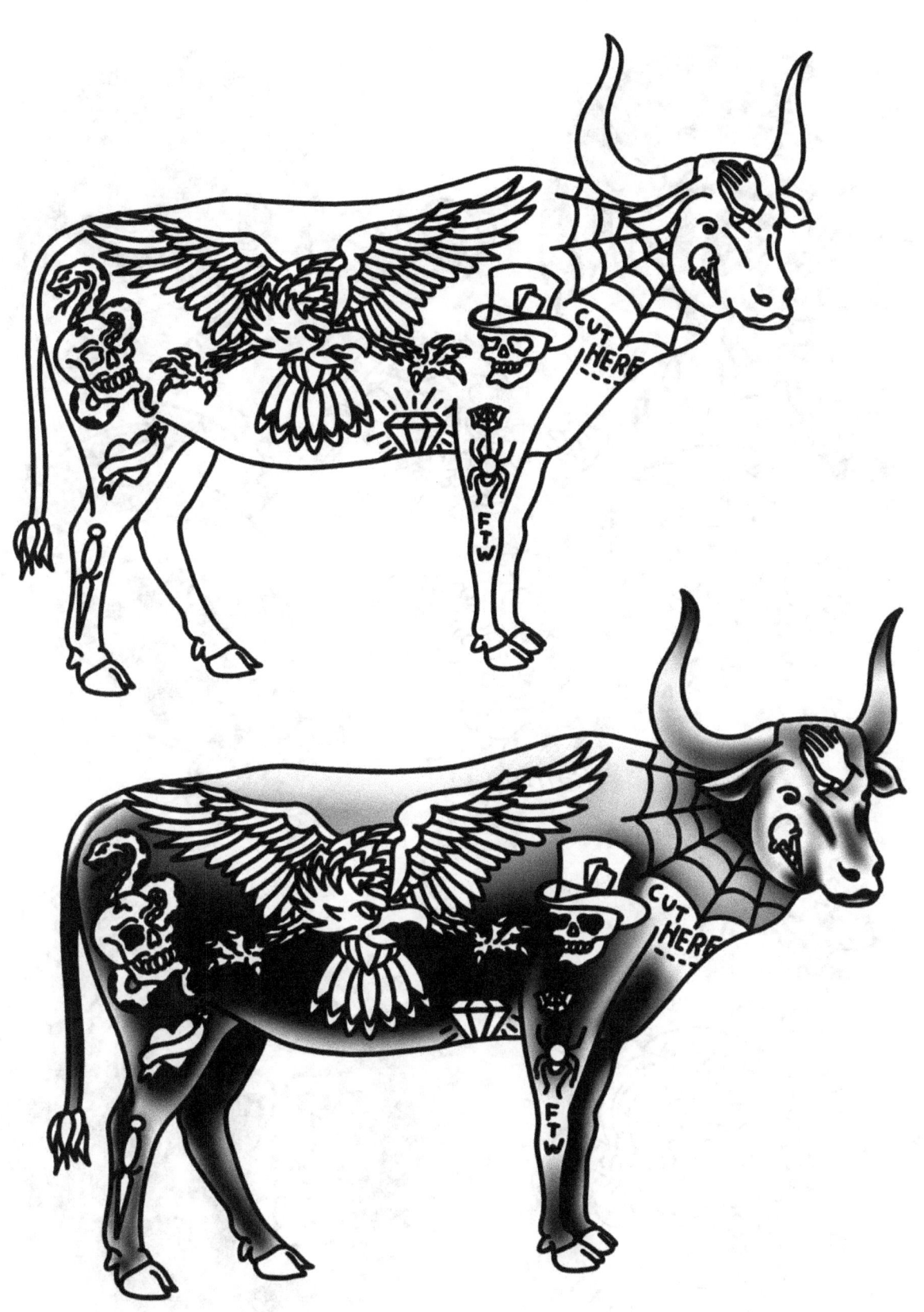

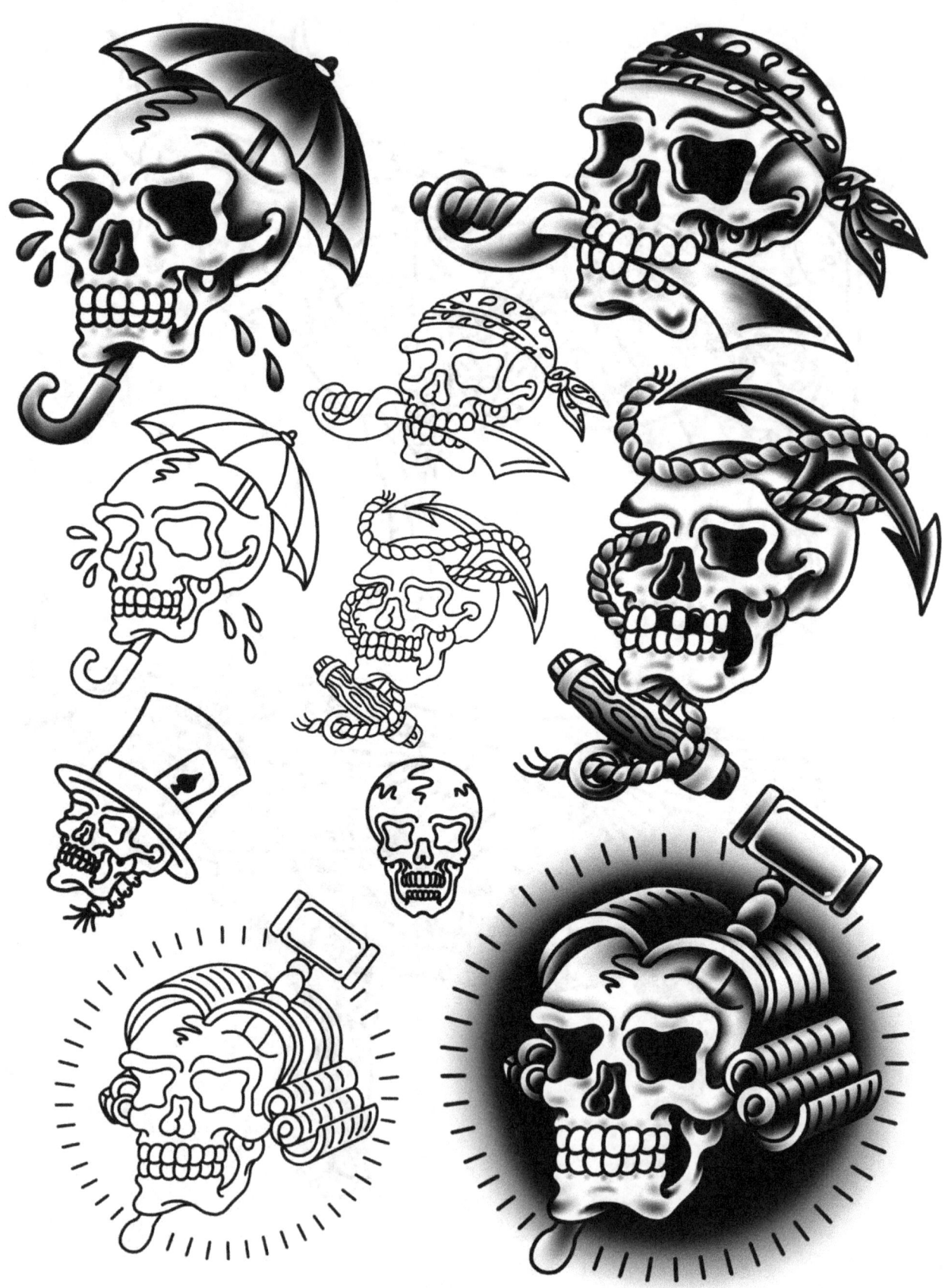

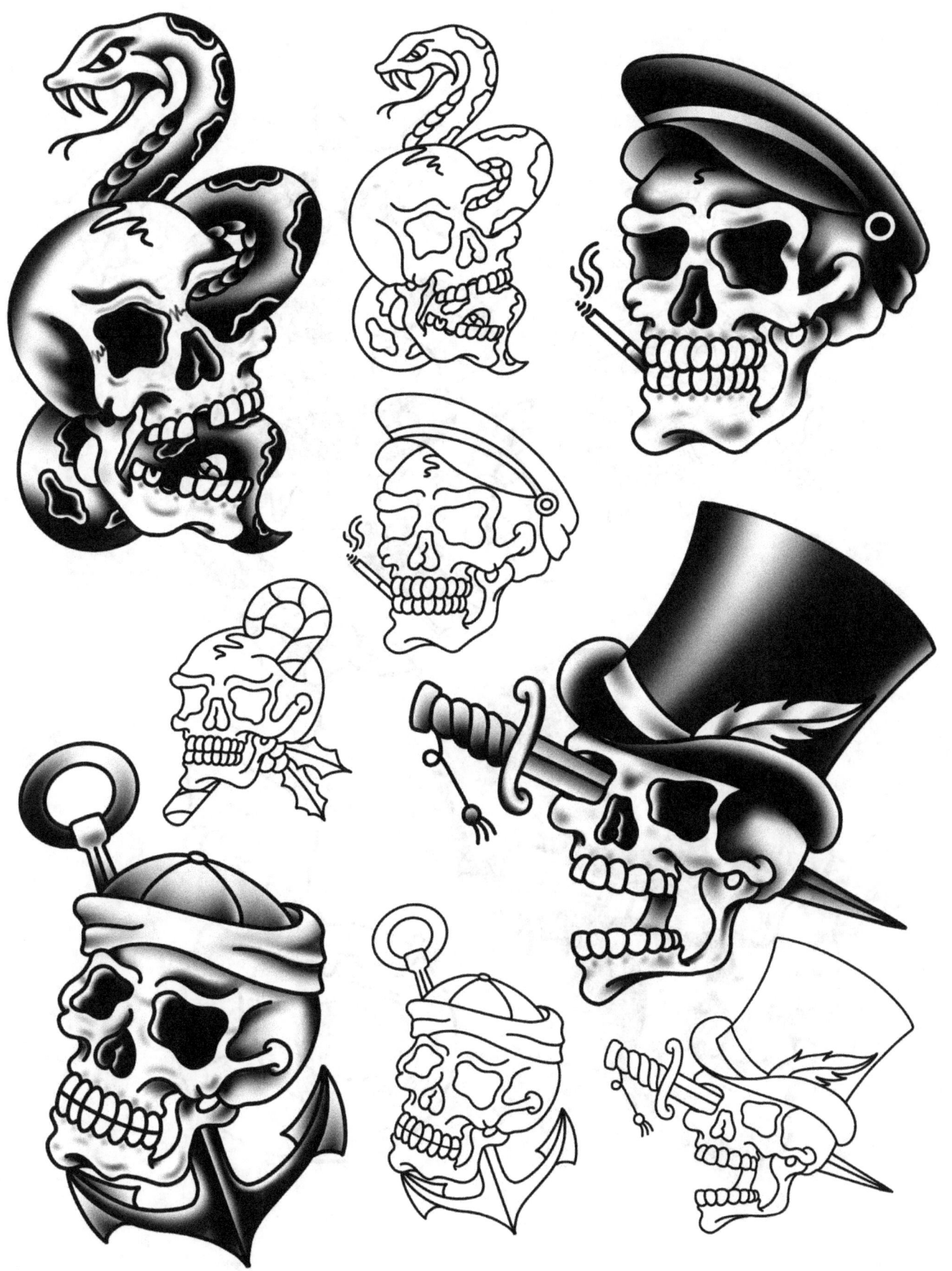

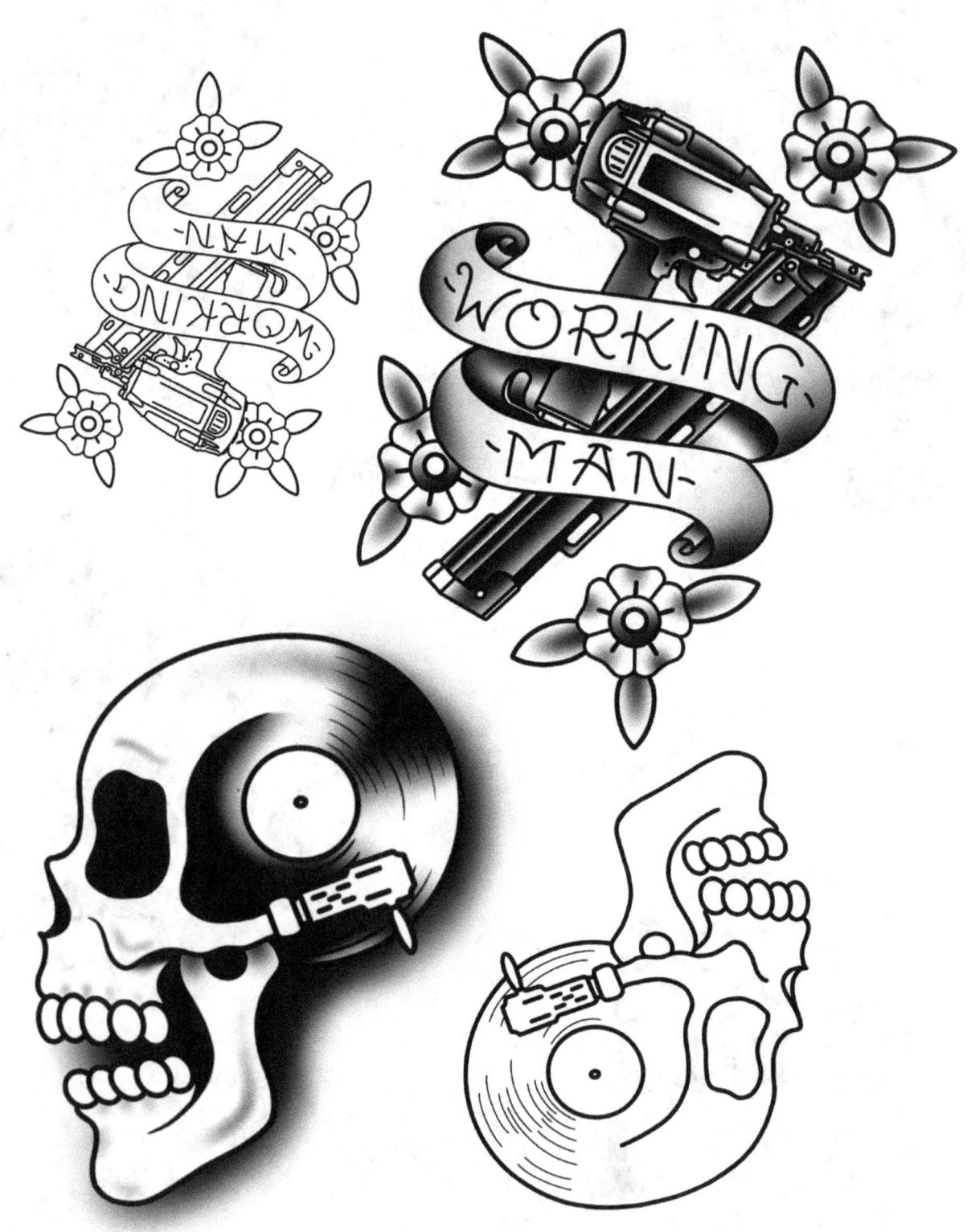

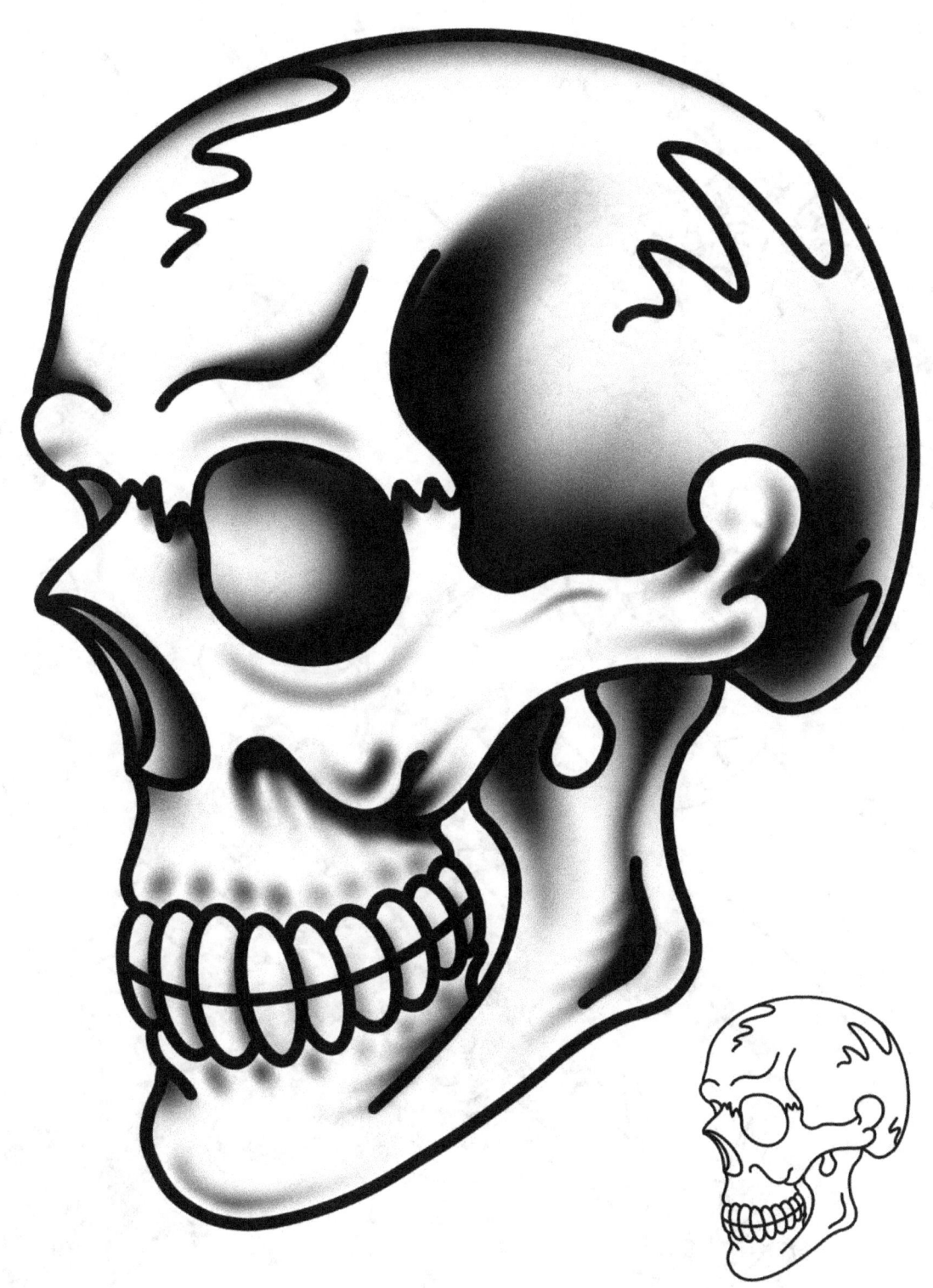

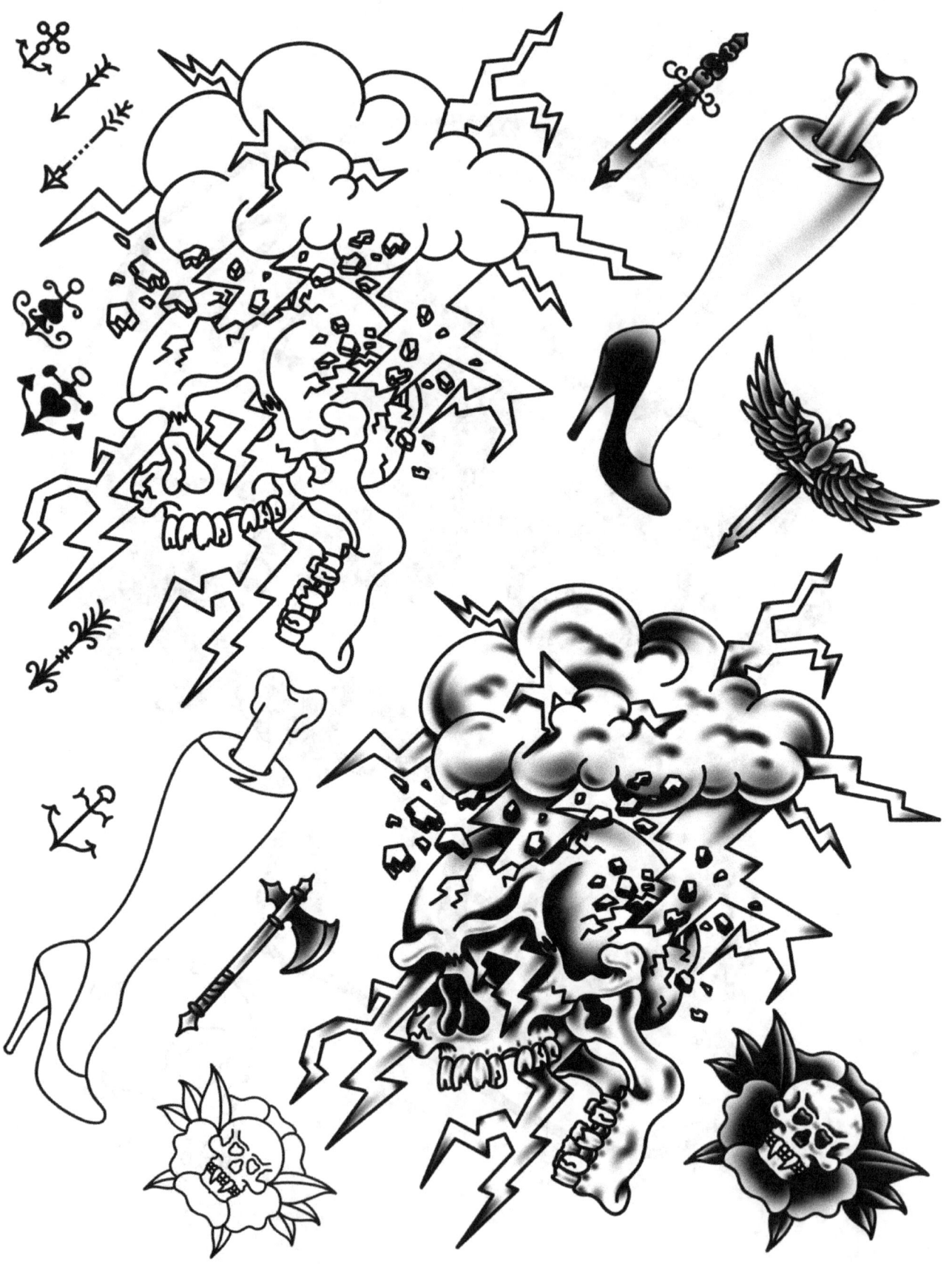

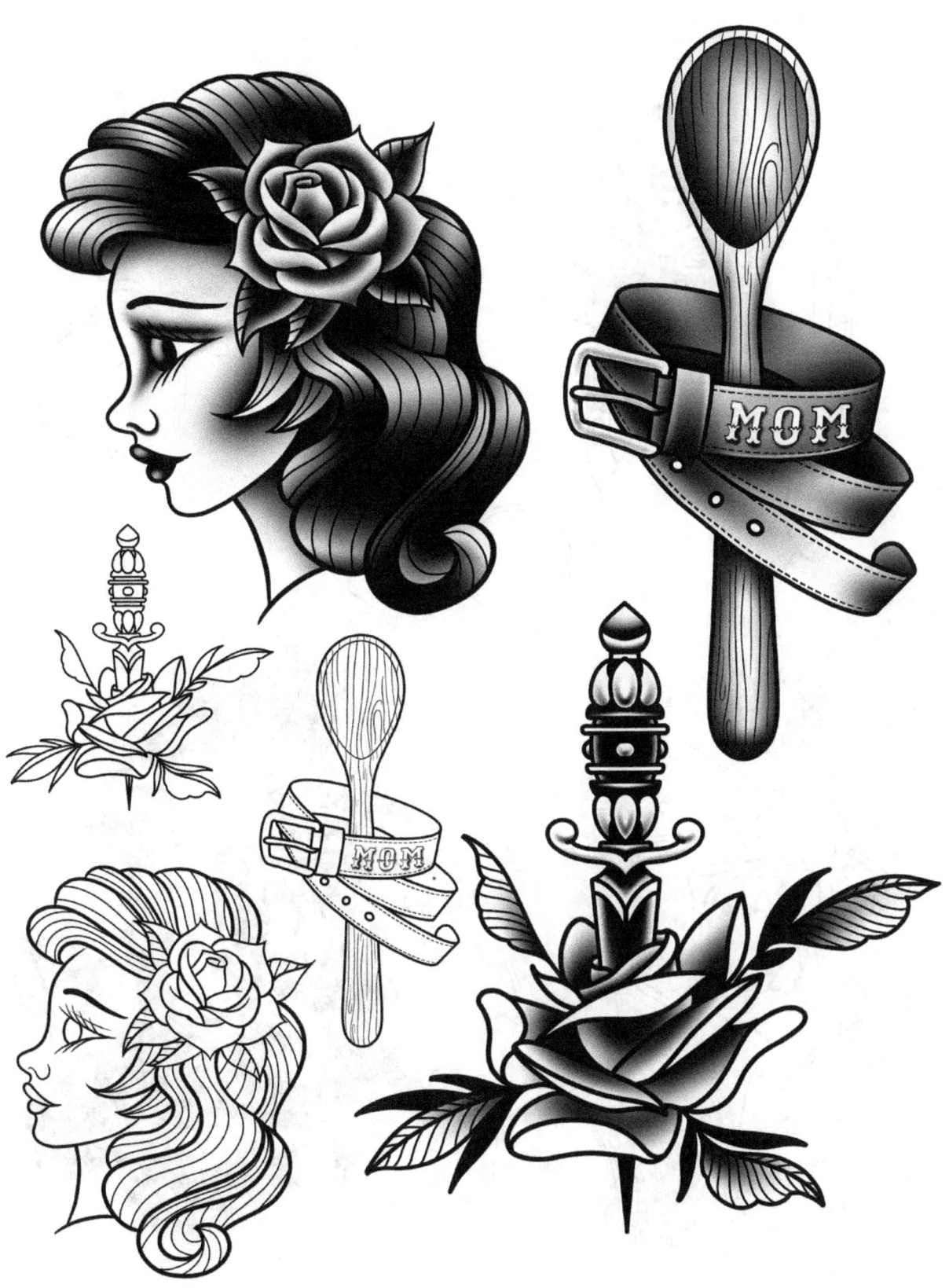

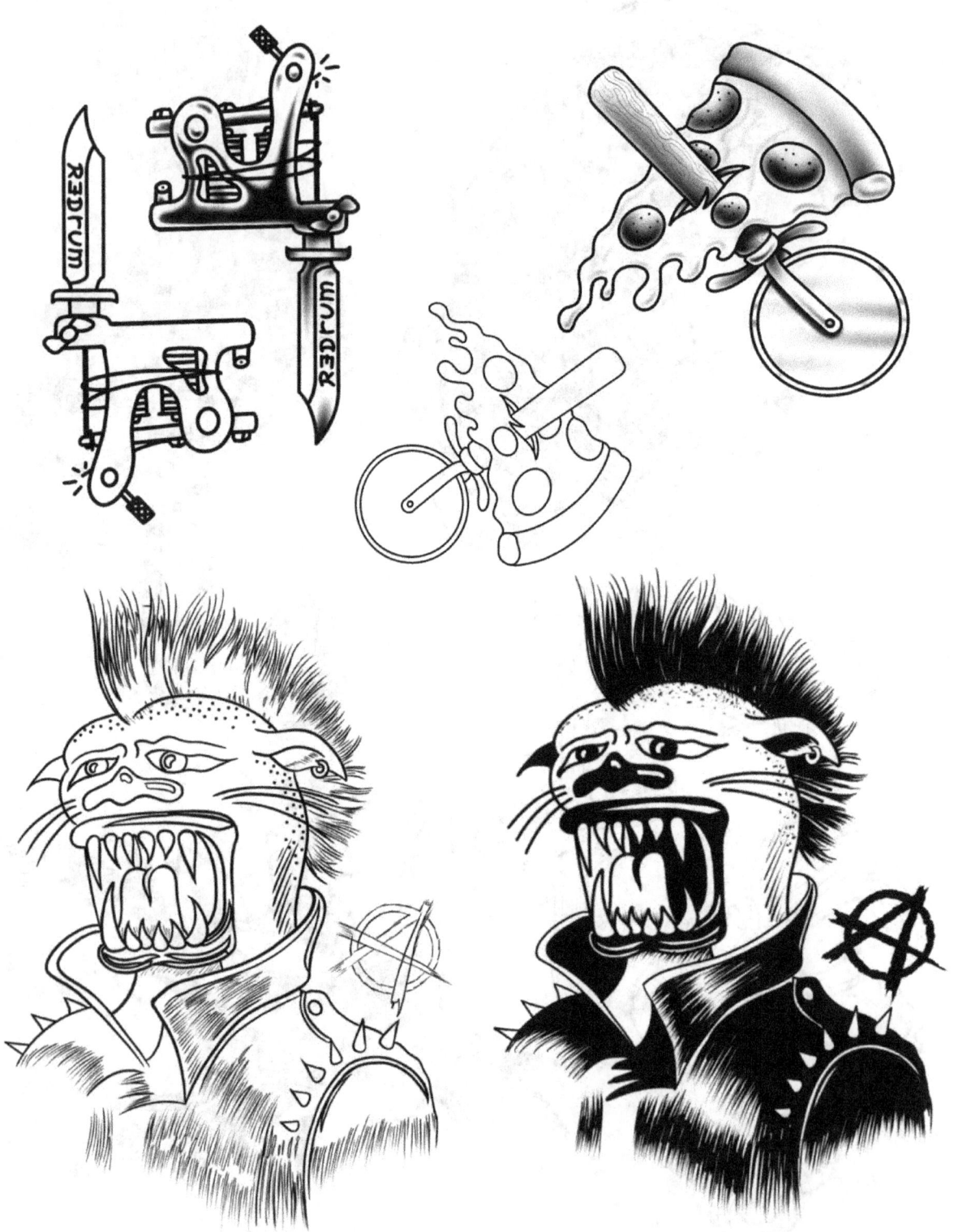

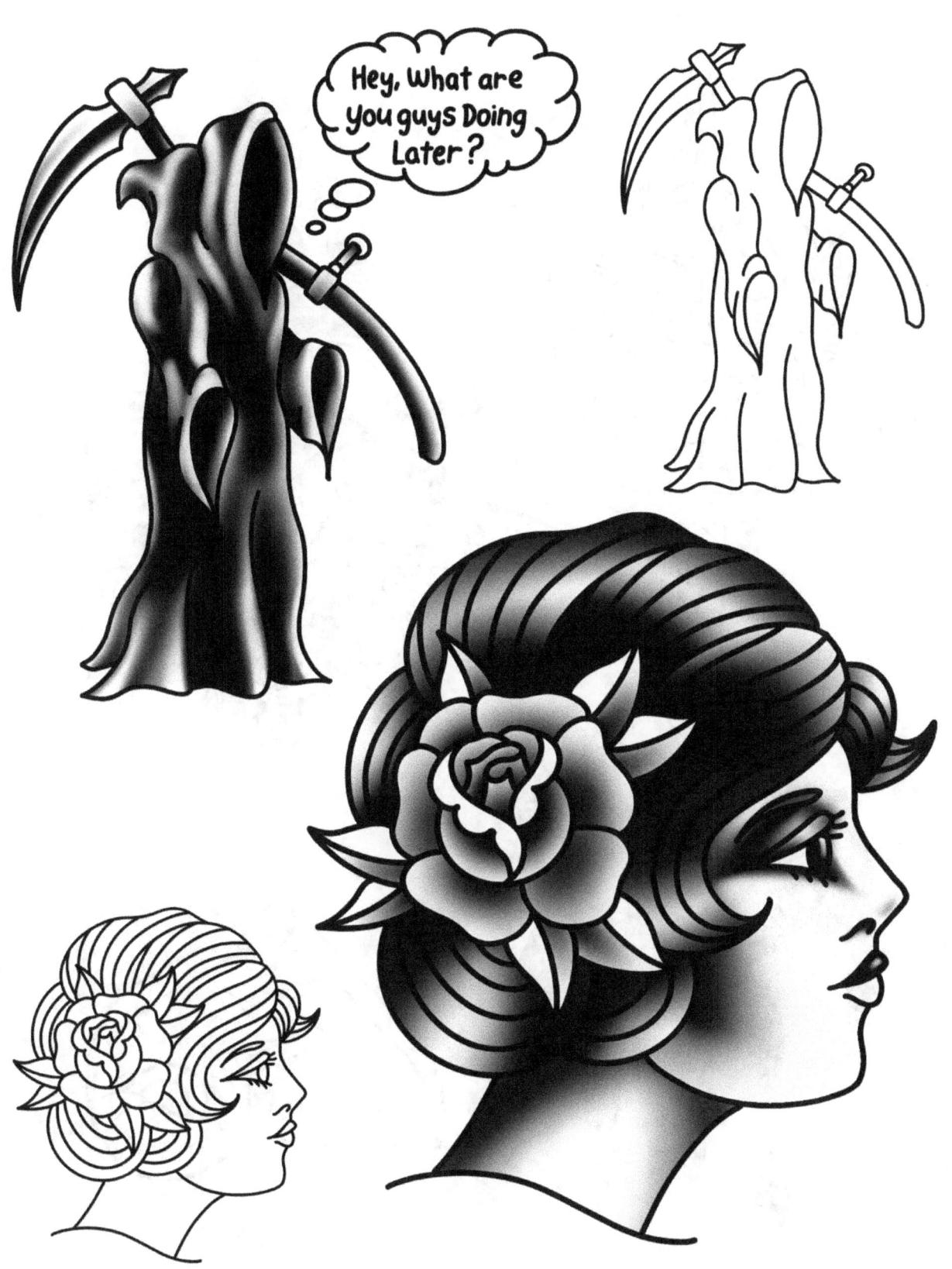

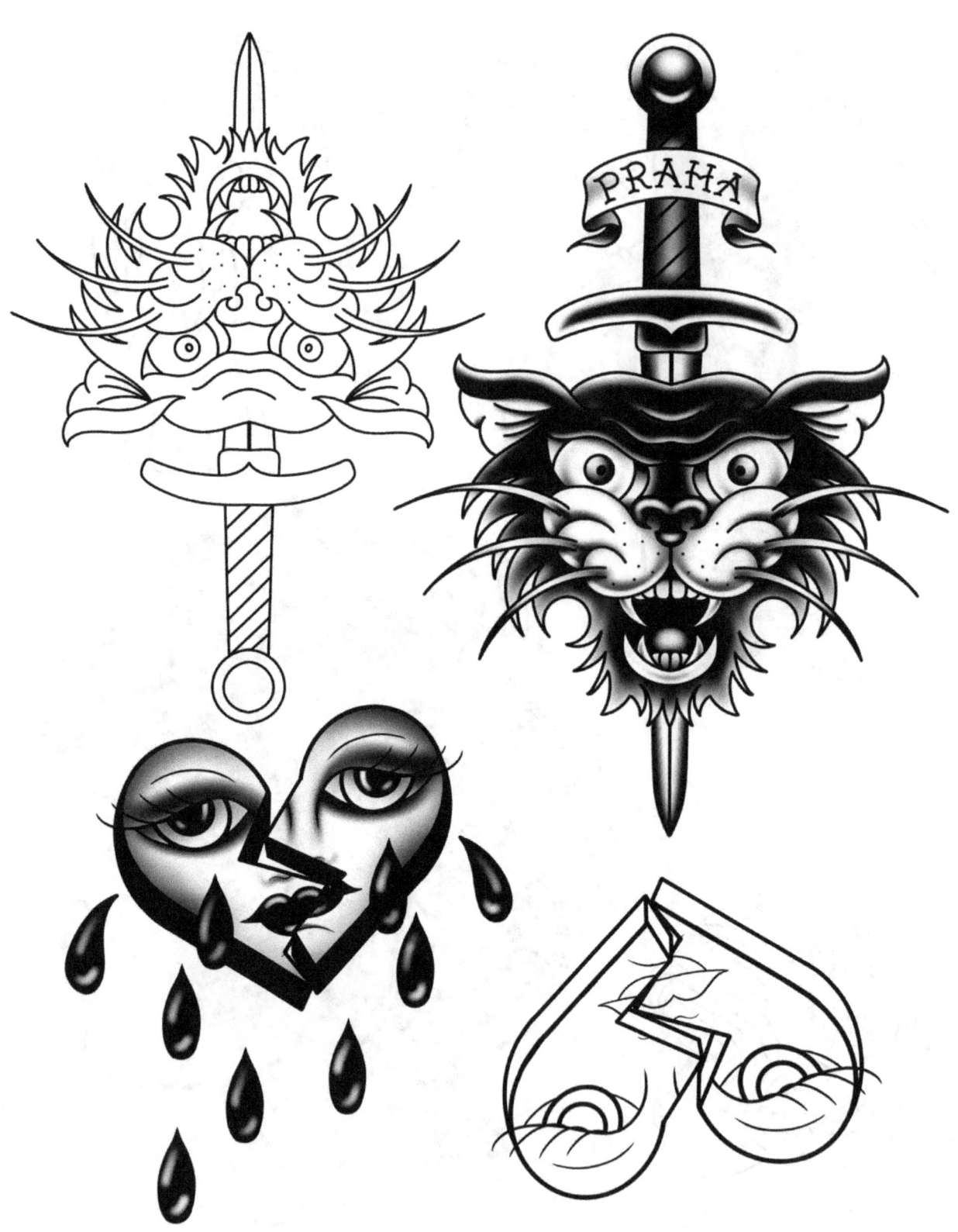

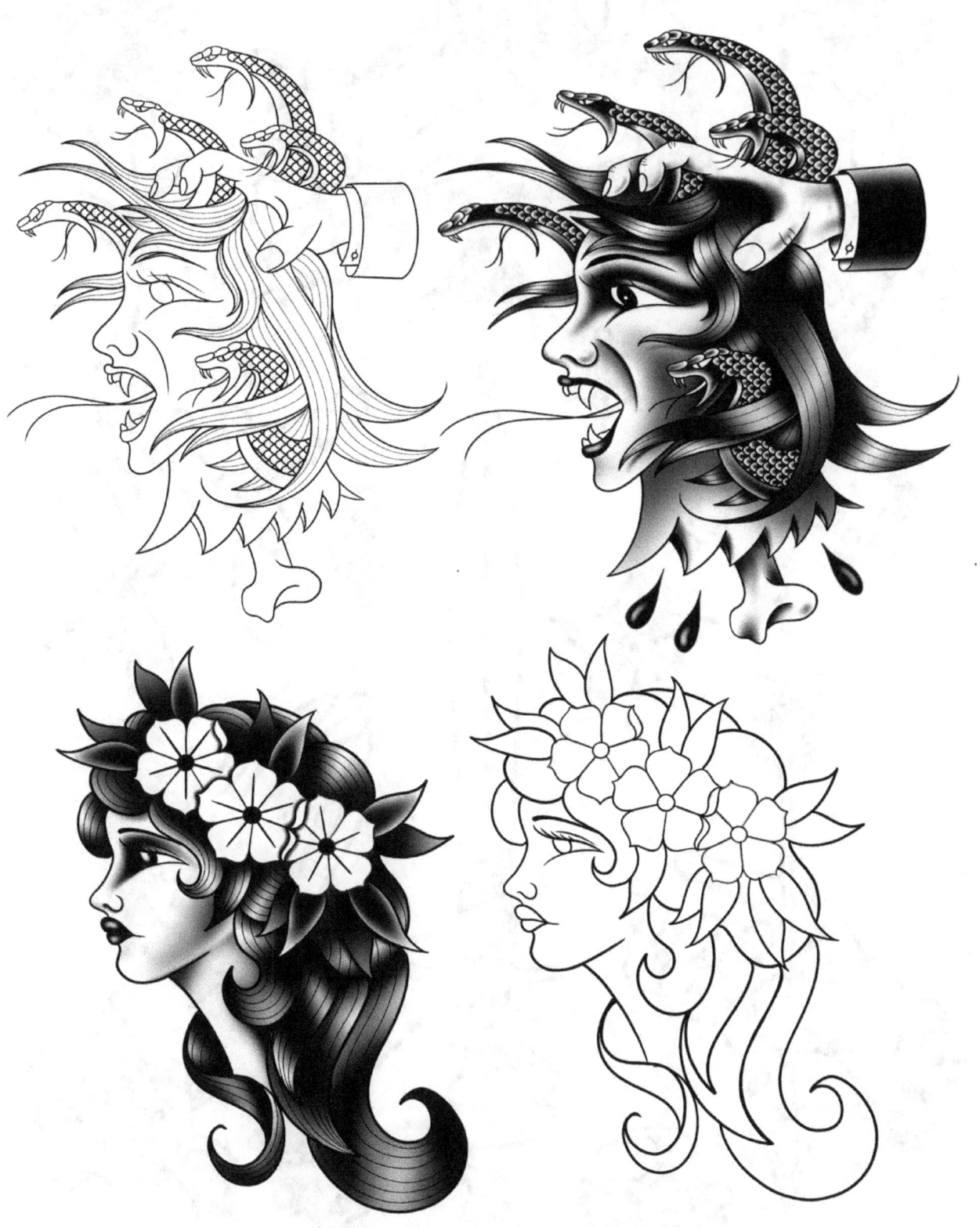

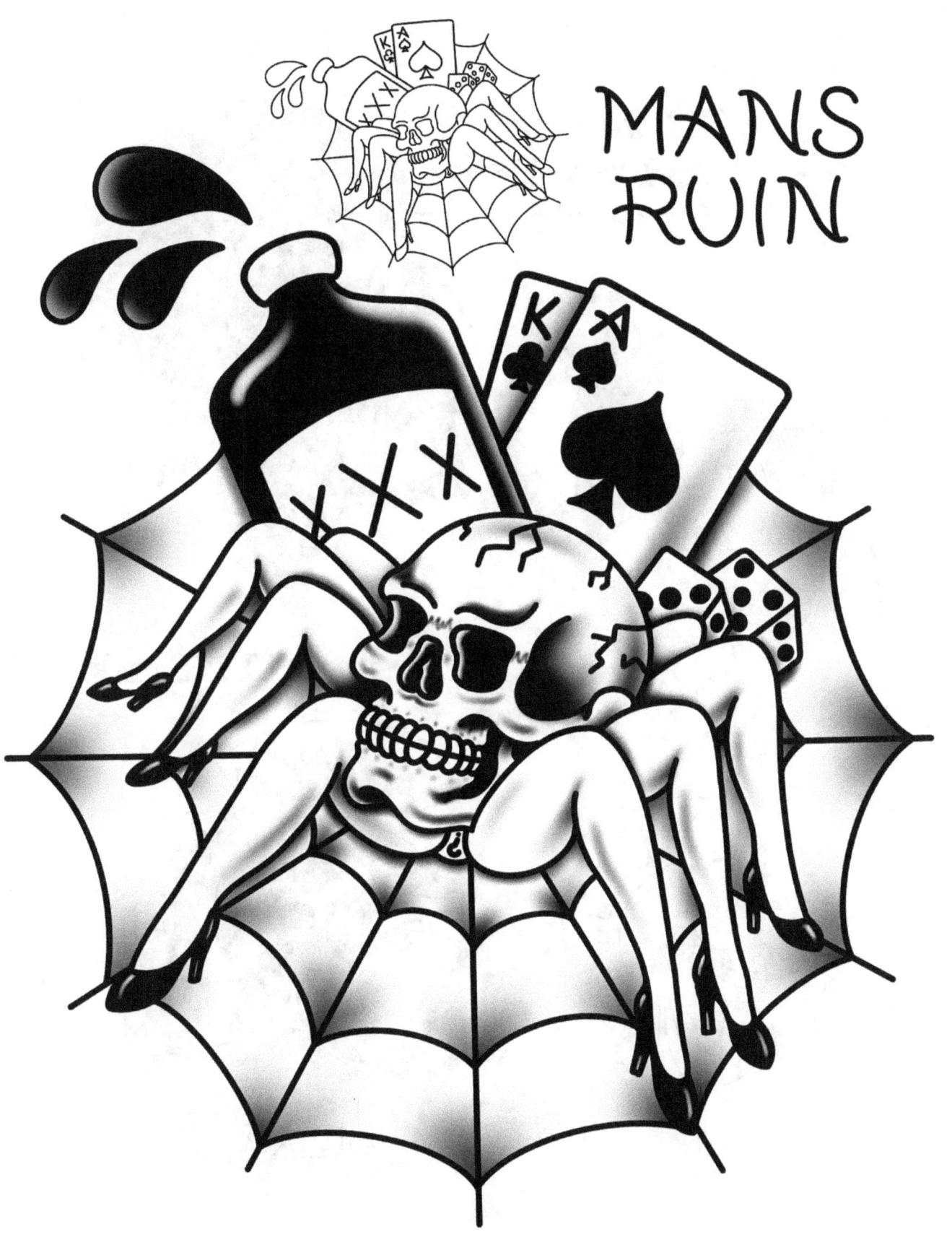

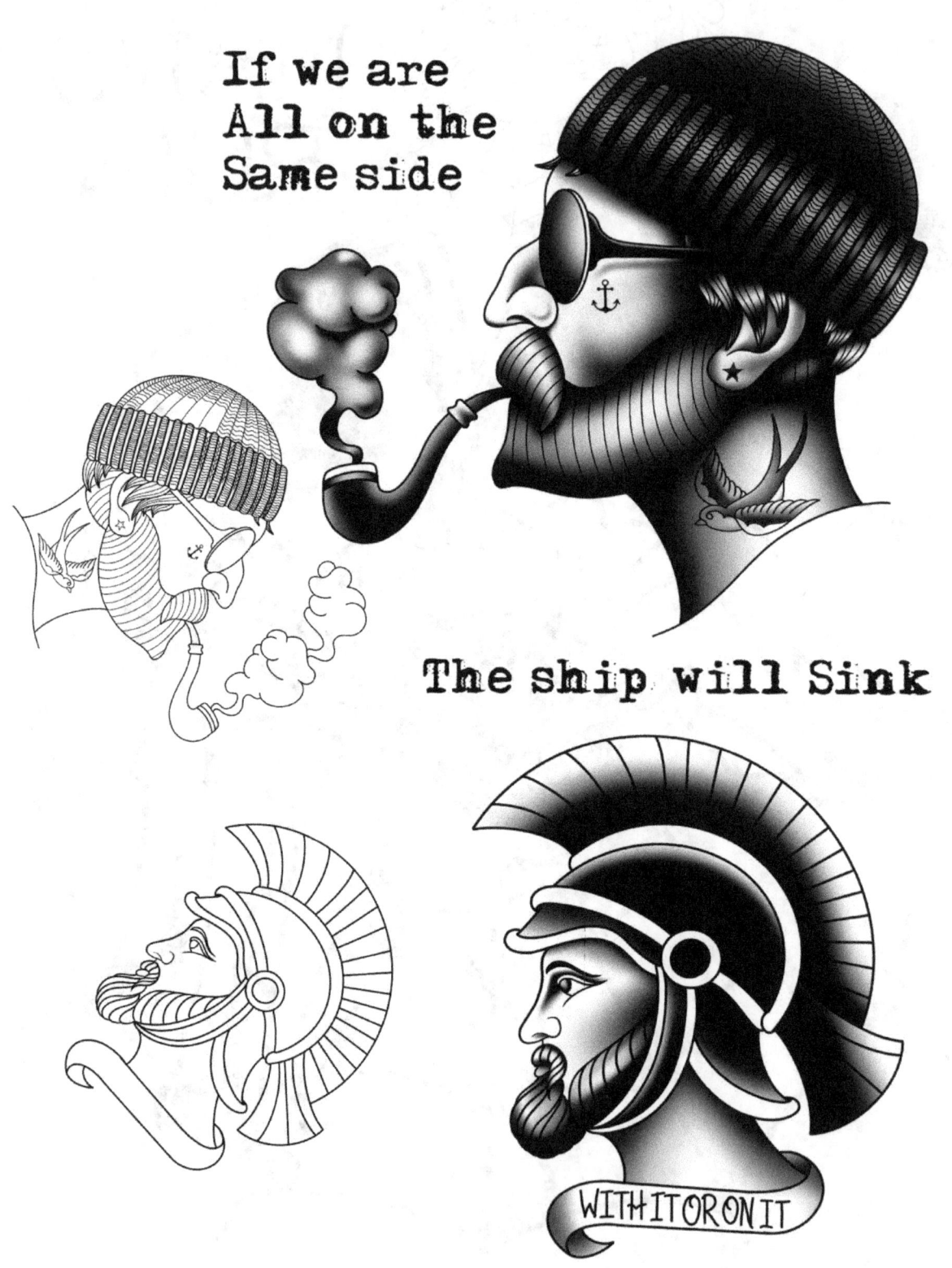

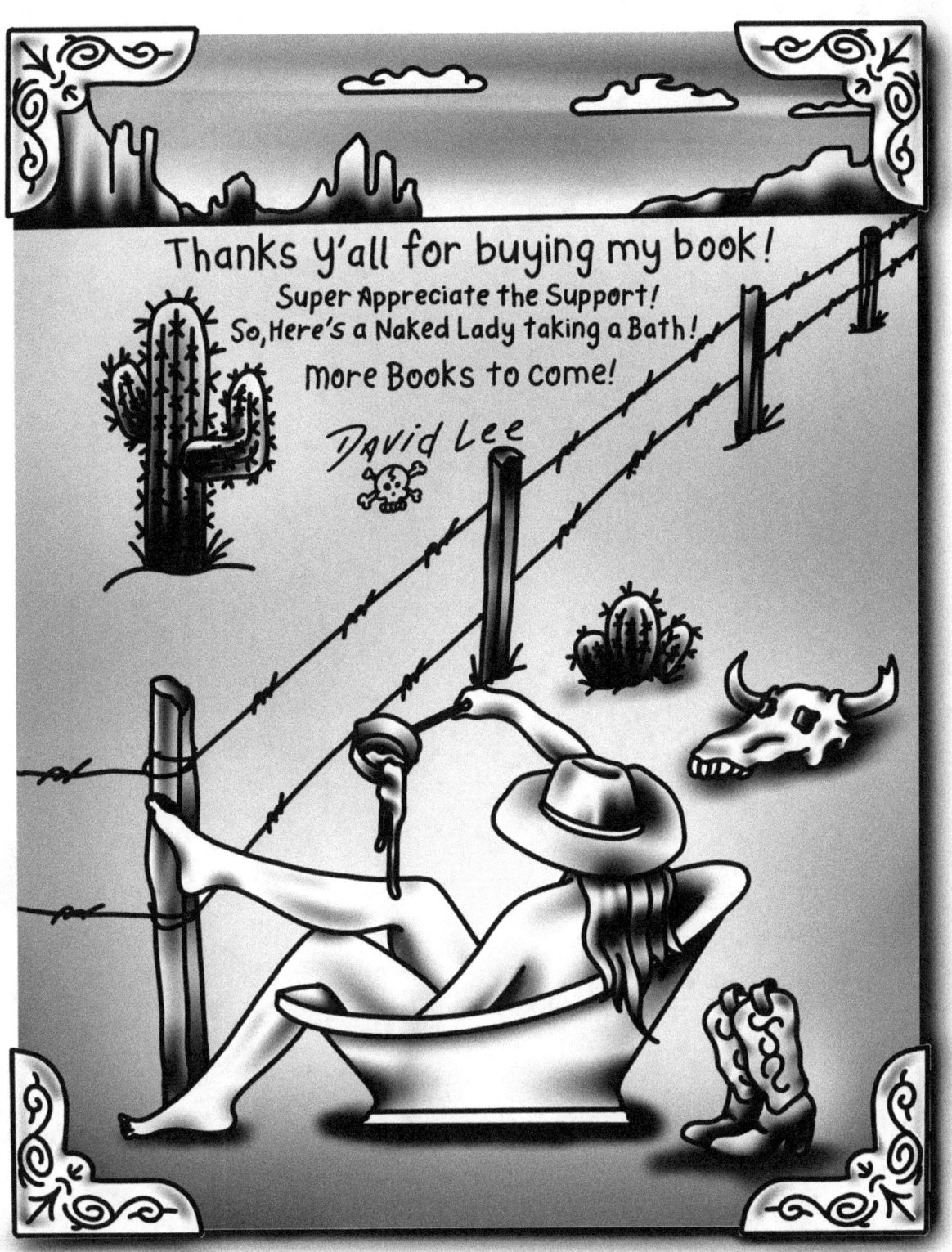

Dogs Don't Like Me is for the ones who carry a little too much in silence - who work their asses off, and laugh just enough to survive the rest.

These poems tackle the hard stuff - death, love, doubt, and what it takes to be a man when nobody's looking.

These poems don't rhyme to be cute, and they're not trying to fix you.

They're just honest, like an old friend telling the truth. *(And sometimes, that's worse.)*

More Shameless Self Promotion

About the author:

David Lee Lough has always had trouble with dogs.
Maybe they don't trust him. Maybe they see a guy who thinks too much and talks too little.

He works a gritty blue-collar job to take care of his wife, his family, and the bills
He writes and draws in whatever times left, because the world doesn't hand you hours, you have to steal them.

If you've ever wondered if anybody else feels the way you do,
this book might be proof that they do.

And if you're married to someone like this…
This might help you understand them better.

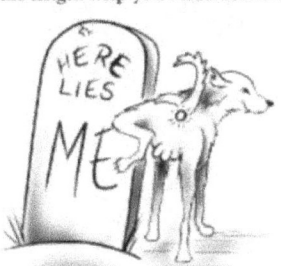

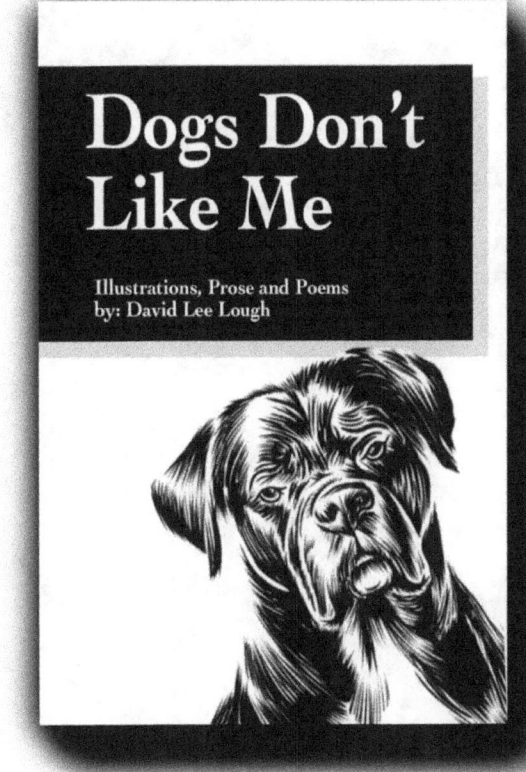

Dogs Don't Like Me is a rough and honest book of poems, prose, and strange little drawings.

It's not tattoo flash.
It's just my poems, rants, and rough sketches about death, love, and why dogs seem to have such a staring problem.

But if you've ever cursed at traffic, argued with God, or felt like people who talk to themselves might not be the weird ones…
you just may be my target audience.

www.ingramcontent.com/pod-product-compliance
Lightning Source LLC
Chambersburg PA
CBHW080535220526
45465CB00006B/2715